CLASSIC SCOTTISH PADDLE STEAMERS

CLASSIC SCOTTISH PADDLE STEAMERS

Alan J. S. Paterson

JOHN DONALD
EDINBURGH

This edition first published in 2002 by
John Donald, an imprint of
Birlinn Limited
West Newington House
10 Newington Road
Edinburgh
EH9 1QS

www. birlinn.co.uk

First published in 1982 by
David & Charles, Newton Abbot

ISBN 0 85976 564 4

British Library Cataloguing-in-Publication Data
A catalogue record for this book is available
from the British Library

Printed and bound by Antony Rowe Ltd, Chippenham, Wiltshire

CONTENTS

INTRODUCTION

Paddle steamers! What nostalgia is evoked by the very thought of those beautiful ships which for generations of holidaymakers were so redolent of summer days at the seaside. Thousands of youngsters have been entranced by cascades of water pouring from wheels revolving mysteriously within gorgeously decorated paddle boxes, or by polished steel connecting rods and crank webs moving purposefully in the hot atmosphere and delectable smells of engine rooms. Many adults have admired the fine lines of one of these vessels, drawing away stern first from a pier amidst her own creaming wake, so irresistibly reminiscent of a bridal train, or perhaps heeling gracefully while swinging towards a quay. Seldom has a specialised class of ship been so aesthetically refined and perfected; sailing ships embraced the famous tea clippers, and ocean liners the celebrated Cunarders, but amongst paddle steamers there were probably more masterpieces contrived in the century and a half of their history than in any other group of steamships.

The end of their story is well nigh in sight, for surviving British paddle steamers can be numbered on the fingers of one hand. All will be out of service in a few years, and it is fitting that the last paddle beats are likely to be heard on or near the Firth of Clyde where, long ago in 1812, the tale began with Henry Bell's *Comet*. It is also an appropriate time for the publication of the story of these well-loved ships and this book explores various aspects of their development from the mid-Victorian period, when the basic modern paddle steamer was rapidly evolving from earlier designs, to the post-war years of our own time. No apology is offered for selecting a series of Scottish vessels as examples for, with few exceptions, the finest practice of each period was found in Clyde and Hebridean waters, granted the claims of the often lovely ships which graced the Bristol Channel, the South Coast and the Thames.

7

These pages therefore describe a variety of Scottish paddle steamers exemplifying the gradual development of modern designs and recalling the different conditions and trades in which these craft operated for many decades. The story begins with the favourite *Iona*, that great Hutcheson veteran which for most of her amazing career of over seventy years was regarded as one of the finest of all excursion vessels. The little known *Chancellor*, sixteen years her junior, typified the best practice of the eighties as well as marking an advance in building techniques; and her useful service on the Clyde was in strong contrast to that of her close contemporary, the ill-starred *Meg Merrilies*, ordered by a railway company in an early attempt to bring new standards of speed and luxury to the tourist trade. The *Grenadier*, one of the most beautiful vessels of her class ever launched, was an interesting example of a ship designed for a dual role, that of Hebridean excursion steamer in summer and Clyde mail vessel during the winter months, and she, together with the North British steamer *Lucy Ashton*, represents general service practice of the later eighties. The latter, one of the most affectionately remembered Clyde paddle steamers of any period, was famous not only for her unusual longevity but also for the remarkable degree of improvement and renewal to which she was subjected during her service under successive railway managements.

The financial resources of Scotland's railway companies permitted lavish new construction during the 1890s, and then and in the ensuing decade the Clyde paddle steamer was developed to high standards of efficiency and beauty. The *Duchess of Hamilton* was one of the best known and possibly the most successful of a number of large cruising paddle steamers intended for summer traffic only, and represented a rare example of this type of ship built for their native firth by the famous Dumbarton firm of William Denny & Bros, better known for their cross-channel ships and, in later years, a splendid series of turbine vessels for the Clyde and other waters. The *Neptune* of the same period was a fine specimen of a paddle steamer intended originally for general railway connections on the Firth of Clyde, but which latterly found excursion work which took her to the outermost limits of the estuary. She, like the *Duchess of Hamilton*, owed her origins to that forgotten genius, Robert

Morton, who did so much to improve British paddle-steamer design.

The *Waverley*, most superb of North British Railway steamers, was a very fine example of a late Victorian cruising vessel from A. & J. Inglis of Pointhouse, whose connection with paddle-steamer design and construction on the Clyde became so close in later years as virtually to exclude other yards. The *Duchess of Fife*, built for the Caledonian Company four years later, was an absolute masterpiece from the Fairfield Company of Govan, and their first Clyde steamer after a magnificent series of large paddle vessels for service on the Thames. Built for general railway work in summer and winter, this attractive ship was the finest example of practical design and aesthetic perfection ever combined in one steamer, and her half century of service testified to the excellence of her construction.

Two Inglis ships of 1910 were designed for different types of work. The *Eagle III*, sub-contracted to other builders, was a late example of a steamer built as cheaply as possible for private owners operating popular 'all the way' sailings from the heart of Glasgow down to the coast. With little money to spare on unnecessary frills, the builders nevertheless produced a handsome, if austere, ship which, after a uniquely chequered career in her early years, eventually settled down as a reliable and well liked Clyde steamer. Her contemporary, the Loch Lomond vessel *Prince Edward*, was for most of her life the largest steamer on that most famous of Scottish lochs and, while having much in common with Clyde ships of the period, also perpetuated traditional practice in the Loch Lomond fleet.

The last ship described is the *Jeanie Deans*, built by the Fairfield Company between the wars. The first of the modern Clyde paddle steamers, her appearance marked the resumption of that form of construction on the firth after a barren fifteen years caused by World War I and subsequent retrenchment. She inaugurated the final generation of Scottish paddle vessels, and her deserved popularity was maintained after 1945 following extensive modernisation and rebuilding at the hands of A. & J. Inglis Ltd. After further service with the railway fleet she was disposed of in 1964, and with her passing from the scene something of the glamour left the Clyde for ever as increasing use of the now ubiquitous car ferries reflected modern trends of diminishing excursion traffic and the preference of a more affluent public for the open road.

Paddle steamers have served their day and generation and are passing from the shipping scene, but theirs has been a long, distinguished, and generally happy history. With them we recall the long, sunny days of boyhood, the carefree holidays of youth, knowing that their disappearance takes with it something of ourselves that we shall never recover. In the pages that follow, however, we may console ourselves with pleasant memories of the graceful ships that have long since sailed beyond our ken.

1

IONA

The Glasgow and Ardrishaig mail run was for many years the most important Clyde passenger steamer service, a fact belied latterly when traffic had fallen away and carriage of the Royal Mail was virtually its sole *raison d'être*. Nevertheless, it had been a trade of major value to its operators during the nineteenth century, when even the railway had still to penetrate the West Highlands and the motor car yet to be invented. A succession of splendid steamers was used on the service, of which the third *Iona* was arguably held in most affection by the travelling public, notwithstanding the immense prestige of her larger consort, the *Columba*. The *Iona*, sailing as she did for over seventy seasons in first-class service, built up a unique reputation in the West of Scotland where she was held in high esteem despite the overpowering presence of the *Columba*, and the variety and interest of her long career are quite unusual in the history of Clyde paddle steamers.

The Royal Route

In the early 1850s, when the brothers David and Alexander Hutcheson acquired from Messrs Burns their West Highland steamboat interests, no railway communication existed between the lowlands and the western seaboard. It was therefore natural that sea transport developed quickly into a network of services analogous to the spread of railways further south, and the difficult nature of the country – broken by sea lochs and studded by islands – indeed favoured steamboats rather than railways. The backbone of the Hutcheson network was the service linking Glasgow and Inverness. Passengers boarded the steamer at the Broomielaw, in the heart of Glasgow, and sailed thence by way of Greenock, Dunoon and Rothesay to the Kyles of Bute and on to the little village of Ardrishaig on Loch Fyne. From this point the Crinan Canal steamer carried them to the edge of the western seas, where another vessel conveyed them north to Oban and Fort William. The final stage of the journey was completed on board the steamer which plied the length of the Caledonian Canal to its destination at Inverness, the Highland capital. Astute advertising seized upon the happy chance of a journey by Queen Victoria to call this the 'Royal Route', and as such it became famous beyond the bounds of Scotland.

So it was that traffic rapidly grew, and the Hutchesons ordered the paddle steamer *Mountaineer* for the Clyde section of the service in 1851. Her very success on the station was her undoing, for traffic swelled so quickly that four years later a larger vessel had to be built to take over and the *Mountaineer* spent the remainder of her career on West Highland services. Her successor on the Ardrishaig route was the first *Iona*, a product of the Govan yard of James and George Thomson.

Iona was typical of the best practice of the period, with flush decks, two funnels, oscillating engines and furnishings of unusually high quality for a river steamer. She would certainly have sailed in the Hutcheson fleet for many years but for the outbreak of the American Civil War in 1861. In an effort to gain an economic stranglehold on the secessionist states of the south, the Federal government immediately imposed a blockade on the Confederacy's seaports in the Gulf of Mexico and on its Atlantic seaboard. Self interest as much as patriotism encouraged the rapid development of a brisk trade by blockade runners who exported southern cotton for sale in Europe and brought back into a predominantly agricultural Confederacy the weapons and machinery which it so desperately needed. The traffic required fast ships and Clyde steamers of the period were ideally suited to the conditions. Accordingly, many of the finest vessels on the firth were disposed of at unusually inflated prices, allowing their fortunate owners to realise handsome profits and build improved ships for the Clyde. The *Iona* was snapped up in 1862, but it was her fate never to reach North America. In dull grey paint she set off on her Atlantic voyage but, having gone no further than Gourock Bay, she was run down and sunk in darkness by a larger ship whose crew had failed to see the unlit steamer gliding across their bows.

Her name was perpetuated by a successor, launched in May

1863 for the Ardrishaig route, a vessel which attracted general admiration as an even finer example of her class than the first *Iona*. The main improvement was the provision of deck saloons fore and aft, but in essence she was a similar type of ship, somewhat modernised, and with more powerful machinery. Entering service in the early summer, she aroused much favourable comment, but her promising career was soon cut short. In July, the hopes of a desperate Confederacy were shattered in a bloody conflict near the little Pennsylvanian town of Gettysburg. The tightening grip on its ports and consequent capture of many blockade runners by Federal cruisers forced the South to make good these losses at any cost; the new Hutcheson flagship was available and was sold to an unnamed purchaser at the end of her first season. She was no more fortunate than her predecessor however, being driven off course by heavy weather and foundering near Lundy Island before her voyage had properly begun.

The Third *Iona*

The Hutchesons went back to J. & G. Thomson for their third Ardrishaig mail steamer in as many seasons, paying for her with the Confederate money received for her short-lived namesake. James and George Thomson became better known as the proprietors of the Clydebank shipyard near Dalmuir, around which grew the present town of that name, but in the 1860s their premises were situated in Govan, on the south bank of the river Clyde. It was there that on the afternoon of 10 May 1864, Master William Hutcheson, nephew of the owners, launched the steamer whose name was already a byword and was destined to be borne by her with distinction for over seventy years.

It might have been expected that a precise repeat of the steamer of 1863 would emerge, but the design was slightly modified and improved. Nevertheless, the resemblance of the third *Iona* to her predecessors reflected the Hutchesons' conservatism. Although equipped with deck saloons her long, low, wrought-iron hull, curved stem, square stern and oscillating machinery characterised her essentially as a steamer of the middle fifties. Comparison with the second ship of the name showed the newer vessel to be slightly longer and beamier, and it was a simple matter to transfer to her the luxurious deck saloons of her namesake which were unnecessary encumbrances in the trade for which she had been intended. These early saloons were really deckhouses and, unlike those of more modern ships, did not form an integral part of the vessel's hull. Being narrower than the main hull, there was room between them and the bulwarks for alleyways at main-deck level, a feature which found some favour on the Clyde in mid-Victorian years. The elegantly finished saloons were widely appreciated when the *Iona* went into service for they represented an immense improvement in a ship of her class, substantially augmenting the meagre covered accommodation of the flush-decked steamers previously employed in Clyde traffic.

The *Iona*'s accommodation was fully described in contemporary newspapers. The *Glasgow Herald*'s correspondent reported:

> The cabin saloon, occupying the after part of the vessel, measures 60 feet in length by 20 feet wide. It is elegantly decorated in white and gold, is provided with cushioned seats of the most luxurious description, and is fitted all round with plate-glass windows, which slide up and down like those of a railway carriage. At the extreme end near the stern a small space is partitioned off, and most tastefully and commodiously fitted up as a ladies' retiring room. Beneath this saloon is the first cabin, a spacious apartment, admirably lighted and ventilated and affording all the comfort of a well-furnished dining room. Immediately adjoining are the steward's pantry, and a gentlemen's retiring room, provided with wash-hand basins and all other needful conveniences. On the forward part of the deck is a second saloon, about 50 feet in length, comfortably fitted up, and affording equally with the other the advantages of shelter from foul weather, abundant light, and perfect ventilation. Below is the second cabin, and between that again and the prow of the vessel is a spacious steerage.

Those familiar with the *Iona* in her later years would probably agree that she was a more beautiful ship then than in her youth, for she was a rare example of a steamer which benefited from later alterations. The main flaws in her original profile were the size and position of the funnels, at once short, stumpy, and placed rather far apart due to the use of horizontal boilers. Her great length was thereby over-emphasised, to the vessel's disadvantage. Nevertheless, the *Iona* was an imposing steamer, beautifully painted and maintained in perfect order. Gilded scrollwork was lavishly employed on bow and stern as well as on the handsome paddle boxes of standard Hutcheson pattern, with five radial vents. Gold lining was carried round hull and sponsons just below main-rail level, and the ship's underbody appears to have been painted pale pink to a few inches above the waterline. Saloons were probably finished in the official 'stone colour' – a creamy shade – which was used until World War I, while the scarlet funnels, black-topped, strikingly complemented the whole. White rails, lifebelts and boats added relief, as did the sail furled to the mast, a feature then part of the standard equipment of Clyde steamers and used regularly in the *Iona*'s case for assisting steering in strong winds. Throughout her long career she flew the well known Hutcheson pennant, the interlaced crosses of Scotland and Ireland on a dark-blue ground, as well as her name pennant and the Royal Mail flag.

The First Decade

The *Iona* was on trial on 18 June 1864 in weather conditions described as unfavourable for a proper test of her capabilities, but she ran the traditional course 'between the lights' – from the Cloch to Cumbrae lighthouses – at an average speed of $19\frac{2}{3}$ statute miles per hour, reckoned to be equivalent to 21 miles per hour in calm weather instead of the south-west gale that she encountered. The general opinion seems to have been that the new ship was not quite as fast as her immediate predecessor, and for the greater part of her life the maximum speed was about $17\frac{1}{2}$ knots.

This splendid steamer entered service on 21 June 1864. Leaving the Broomielaw at seven o'clock in the morning, she called at Custom House Quay, Greenock, to uplift passengers from Glasgow by the Caledonian Railway, and proceeded thence to Rothesay with intermediate calls at Kirn, Dunoon and Innellan. After Rothesay, calls were made at Colintraive and Tighnabruaich in the Kyles of Bute before the *Iona* rounded Ardlamont Point and entered Loch Fyne. There was no adequate jetty at Tarbert in those days, passengers being put ashore by ferry, and the steamer's outward run ended at Ardrishaig just after midday. Following a brief interval of some forty minutes she retraced her route to Glasgow, arriving in the city in the early evening.

Never deviating from her regular route, save for the addition of a call at the new Glasgow & South Western railhead at Prince's Pier, Greenock, from its opening in 1869, the *Iona* speedily built up a reputation as the Clyde's first favourite. An extract from a popular Glasgow magazine of the time conveys something of her unique standing in the eyes of the public:

> Our most celebrated steamer is the world-renowned Iona, 'gay, and fresh, and fair', pleasant to look upon, and surrounded in every one's recollection with pleasant associations. When we think of the delights of a joyous summer tour in the West Highlands, the prelude to our thought is the sail in the Iona. The very name of the ship is fraught with poetry and music – it carries in its note an Ossianic whisper of the isles by the sounding seas. A tourist can scarcely be said to have graduated as a tourist until he has enjoyed the delights of the passage to Ardrishaig.

Attention has often been drawn to the wide differences in social class in Victorian times, and the *Iona*, above all her contemporaries, enjoyed the status of a 'society' boat, in which landowners, their families and guests travelled to and from the West Highland estates. Consequently, the facilities and standard of comfort provided on board in the first-class accommodation in those days were far in advance of the plainer and often spartan conditions obtaining in modern one-class ships of the car ferry type, although it must be conceded that the luxury available to better off Victorians was usually ensured at the expense of low wages and long working hours on the part of the lower orders including, no doubt, the Hutcheson employees. Nevertheless, modern ideas of social justice troubled few minds in the 1860s and a first-class traveller in the *Iona* was free to take advantage of such facilities as a bath, a fruit stall, and a post office in addition to the many other comforts of the Clyde's premier excursion steamer.

Several of the *Iona*'s crew remained with the ship for many years and became firm favourites with passengers. Perhaps the best known in the early years was John Murray, the young and very popular purser, whose death in 1874 was mourned by a

wide circle of friends and acquaintances who contributed
generously towards a monument at his grave in the Argyllshire
village of Taynuilt, inscribed:

John Murray, late Purser of the Royal Mail Steamer
Iona, born 27th August, 1839, died 29th November, 1874.
This stone was placed by a number of West Highland
gentlemen, in testimony of their respect and esteem
for one whose amiability of character and active
efficiency made him a universal favourite, and whose
early death is much regretted.

Improvements and Alterations

The steamer was subjected to a thorough renovation by her
builders in 1875, one of several overhauls which kept her well
abreast of contemporary standards and prolonged her career far
beyond the ordinary span. The *Iona* was virtually gutted; very
little remained except the hull and engines, and the former was
greatly strengthened. Although no details are available, it may
reasonably be supposed that additional bulkheads were
provided. The boilers were replaced by new ones of similar type
and the engine room henceforth was open to view from the main
deck. The navigating bridge, an improvement which had been
added in time for the 1871 season, was enlarged by a rearward
extension along the roof of the ticket office and the steam-
steering engine being transferred to the engine room. The *Iona*
had been fitted with steam steering in 1873, the first Clyde vessel
to be so equipped, and this device must have eased considerably
the task of Donald Leitch, her well known pilot, in controlling the
long, slim hull in difficult conditions of wind and tide. Many
other improvements were carried out in the course of bringing
the ship up to date, and the *Iona* was finally fully repainted in
time for trials early in May 1875 when she ran the lights at an
average speed of 22 statute miles per hour, an improvement upon
her original performance in 1864.

Her reputation was understandably of a high order but
'Hatan', a regular contributor to the long defunct *Oban
Telegraph*, took a humorous view of the smart uniforms worn by
the crew of this crack steamer and in the summer of 1877 wrote:

Who does not weary of City Life? I yesterday invested some odd shillings in a trip to Ardrishaig to advantage. You have likely heard of the Iona. Splendid steamer. But did it ever strike you the tremendous amount of brass on board. The captain [John McGaw] wears a uniform of brass on blue ground of cloth, and a brass cap. It is a sweet sight to see the clerk all clad in brass, mount a plate, and be served round like – by the bos'n, to collect the fares. The sight once seen will haunt you till your dying day . . . I was bedazzled with brass – bedazzled with brass to such an extent that I cannot fix my eye on a door-plate without a shiver. The company could surely afford to give its servants buttons of gold, and I know the servants would not be too proud to wear them; but to be bedazzled with brass is preposterous. The sun on a summer's noon is not half so resplendent as the second steward, and Solomon in all his glory could not hold a candle to the cook. There are more brass buttons on board the Iona than there are stars in heaven. I am afraid I won't get over that brass in a hurry. The glitter and glare have upset me completely.

In view of the expensive modernisation in 1875, the *Iona*'s career as principal steamer of the Hutcheson fleet might well have been thought secure for many more seasons, but the advent of an imposing rival in 1877 brought about her premature replacement as flagship. Formation of the Glasgow & Inveraray Steamboat Company and the inauguration of a daily service from Glasgow to the head of Loch Fyne with the magnificent *Lord of the Isles* resulted in competition at all the Hutcheson calling places except Tarbert and Ardrishaig so that, splendid steamer though she was, the *Iona* lost traffic to the newcomer. David MacBrayne, for many years a partner of the Hutcheson brothers, was then about to assume full control of the firm – he ran it under his own name from 1879 – and his initiative resulted in the appearance of the superb *Columba* from J. & G. Thomsons' new Clydebank yard in 1878. The finest Clyde steamer of that and perhaps any period, she quite outranked the *Lord of the Isles* and secured the Ardrishaig trade for her owners. In fact there was a growing traffic on this popular tourist route, and not only was the *Lord of the Isles* able to keep a profitable share but the Hutcheson service was doubled by retention of the *Iona* in 1878–9 to provide an extra service between Glasgow and Ardrishaig.

Completion of the Callander & Oban Railway in the early

summer of 1880 brought about the transfer of the *Iona* to West
Highland waters. Although circuitous and slow by later
standards, the new train service offered a faster journey to Oban
than MacBrayne's 'Royal Route' and there can be little doubt
that the *Iona* was sent north to provide a more luxurious vessel
on the Oban–Fort William section than the *Mountaineer*, a
steamer much her senior and considerably inferior in
accommodation. Ships of the standard of the *Columba* and *Iona*
could reasonably be expected to offer an attractive alternative to
the new railway and, as events proved, the MacBrayne route not
only retained its trade but drew increased traffic. The *Iona* spent
a short time on the Ardrishaig service before sailing north at the
end of June, in time for the opening of the railway. Her arrival
was something of an event as she 'steamed gracefully into Oban
bay, decked with bunting, and signalling her arrival by the
discharge of two guns. On reaching the North Pier, which was
crowded with an expectant multitude, eager to view the popular
craft, she was greeted with ringing cheers.'

There is no doubt that the steamer offered a very high quality
of accommodation. Amongst other facilities she boasted a post
office, but an entirely new feature was the provision of gasoline
lighting, which offered a more brilliant, if harsher, source of
illumination than oil lamps. 'Nothing could be more inviting
than the saloon with its white and gold decorations, its warm red
curtains, and luxurious lounges, while the dining cabin, with its
rich furnishings, and bouquets of fresh cut flowers, is equally
attractive.' Thus reads the *Oban Times* of that period, the
columns of which faithfully reflected the rapidly growing
importance of the little West Highland town at the centre of an
expanding tourist trade.

When the new *Grenadier* joined the fleet in 1885 the *Iona*
returned to the Clyde to give a supplementary service daily
between Ardrishaig and Glasgow, lying overnight at the former
port and leaving for the city at 6.30 in the morning, returning
from the Broomielaw at 1.45pm. During late spring and in the
autumn she replaced the *Columba* when traffic was too light to
justify employment of the larger steamer, but before it settled to
the winter level at which it could be handled adequately by the
Grenadier. Captain John McGaw had by this time been forced to
retire due to poor health and both *Iona* and *Columba* had begun

their association with another celebrated master, Angus Campbell – an association which continued until his death at the end of 1903.

In 1889 the *Iona* was due for further renovation. No expense was ever spared to ensure that she was turned out in the finest condition and her annual overhauls were supplemented at longer intervals by major reconstruction, but at this time there appears to have been some doubt as to her future and she lay out of service during the whole of 1890. Rumour was current that she might be replaced by the *Victoria*, a modern saloon paddle steamer built in 1886 for railway connections out of Wemyss Bay and available for purchase following a reorganisation of services from that port, but David MacBrayne opted for a complete rebuilding of the *Iona*. Hutson & Corbett of Kelvinhaugh received the contract for overhaul and reboilering, the work involving replacement of the vessel's horizontal navy boilers by two 'haystacks' – the classic form of Clyde steamer boiler since the sixties.

The change seemed retrograde, for navy boilers were at last beginning to be used generally for new ships in other fleets and David MacBrayne's decision to specify the older type was thought strange. Later reboilering of other steamers with haystack boilers indicated a consistent policy, however, and suggested that the navy type was too short-lived to be economical: the *Iona*'s first set lasted about twelve years and their replacements not much longer, but the 1891 boilers had a much longer life. They were better steamers, and substantially lighter than the older boilers, so that the *Iona*'s draught was reduced by fully six inches after alteration. Aesthetically, the change was for the better. The funnels, now lengthened, were moved closer together, adding grace and elegance to the steamer's profile.

Mechanically, *Iona* was improved by the substitution of a surface condenser for the jet type and, after a comprehensive refurbishing and repainting, she ran trials on the Skelmorlie mile on 6 June 1891, achieving a speed of 17.143 knots. By a curious coincidence her return to the Clyde took place in the same year as the departure of her old rival, the *Lord of the Isles*, sold to the Thames on replacement by a new vessel of the same name.

Golden Jubilee

The *Iona* remained on the Clyde until the outbreak of World War I, supplementing the summer sailings of the *Columba* and for brief periods in spring and autumn standing in for the larger vessel on the Ardrishaig mail service. Wemyss Bay became the railhead for the older ship, which lay overnight at Ardrishaig and early in the present century regularly undertook a very taxing timetable. Leaving before six o'clock every morning she sailed to Wemyss Bay, making the usual calls at Tarbert and Kyles of Bute piers. She then returned with Caledonian Railway passengers directly to Ardrishaig, arriving there approximately at the same time as the *Columba* from Glasgow. On one or two days she fitted in a short cruise to Loch Fyne before her afternoon return sailing to Wemyss Bay. For a ship then over forty years old it was a demanding schedule but it was done without fuss, year after year.

The fine old steamer celebrated her golden jubilee in the early summer of 1914, but for the *Iona* and her crew there was no celebration – simply a case of 'business as usual', in the words of a later generation. A correspondent of the *Glasgow Herald*, writing on her anniversary in May, 'looked for some outward sign of decorative triumph as the old steamer passed my window this morning, but there was nothing to show that she had completed her jubilee beyond her smart appearance'. The *Iona* was then on the Greenock and Ardrishaig mail run, a whole day's sail from Glasgow by third-class rail and cabin class in the steamer being advertised for as little as 7s; with breakfast, dinner and tea inclusive, the day's outing could be had for only 10s.

A less happy incident in her jubilee summer occurred early in July when the *Iona* was involved in one of her rare accidents, during her inward run from Ardrishaig. Approaching Rothesay pier, the steamer's path was partially obstructed by large numbers of yachts being swung shorewards at their moorings by an east wind, and the upshot was that she collided with the quay, cutting three feet into the timbers and denting her bow plating. Fortunately there were no injuries, but the affair illustrated the navigational hazards of Clyde steamer operation when the firth was at the peak of its holiday popularity in those spacious years before World War I.

Changed Days

The outbreak of war brought many changes to the Clyde and gradually passenger services were whittled away to a bare minimum. Most of the modern steamers were taken by the Admiralty for naval duties, and responsibility for maintaining services devolved upon older ships such as the *Iona*. She herself, even apart from her age, was quite unsuited for war work, and her contribution throughout those bleak years was to maintain services from Wemyss Bay, at first on the Ardrishaig route but, from 1916, on charter to the Caledonian Steam Packet Company to keep up its Rothesay connections. The vessel had been painted grey, but at this period wore the all-yellow funnels of the railway subsidiary.

In the winter of 1918–19 she was renovated and given new saloons of the old design, extending about ten feet further forward, to reappear in the first post-war summer in all her old finery. In truth she seemed ageless, one of the few survivors of happier years in a changed world. In 1922 she was transferred to a new station, sailing from Glasgow to Lochgoilhead during the summer, and this was continued for six years until, in 1928, she returned to West Highland service which she had last undertaken in Queen Victoria's time. Based at Oban during the summer months, she maintained the Fort William service and there remained for the rest of her long career, acting as deputy to the *Columba* on the Ardrishaig route in spring and autumn as hitherto. Latterly, therefore, her Clyde presence was limited and she became really a West Highland steamer, being laid up at Greenock during the winter months. During the high season, however, she became as much of an institution on the Loch Linnhe route as she had been over forty years before.

Old-fashioned by now she certainly was, but the classical beauty of her long hull, the rich colours of the MacBrayne funnels, and the smartness of her appearance made an unforgettably dignified and striking impression, especially against the backcloth of some of the finest scenery in the western highlands. It was in these waters and, alas, too young to appreciate the fact, that your author made the first voyages of his life on board the *Iona*, and nostalgia for them has very largely prompted this chapter.

Lochaber no More

On an early spring day in 1936 I stood for the last time on the deck of the *Iona* as she lay in the dock of Arnott, Young & Co (Shipbreakers) Ltd at Dalmuir. She and her great consort, the *Columba*, had been withdrawn at the close of the previous summer, to the widespread regret of all who had known them. Few could imagine the Clyde without the magnificent veterans. The *Iona* had sailed for seventy-two years, a record unlikely to be approached by any more modern ship. When she was new, the American Civil War was still in progress, Louis Napoleon was Emperor of France and Bismarck had not yet achieved the unification of Germany; in her last months, a Europe only recently recovered from the ravages of World War I was under new threat from Hitler's Third Reich. What a difference lay between the worlds of her youth and old age, between the high noon of the Victorian era and the uncertainties of the 1930s.

In her seven decades of sailing gracefully on her native Clyde, the *Iona* had earned the respect and affection of generations of Glasgow people, and it was truly said on her departure from the firth that her like would never be seen again. In the whole history of Clyde steamers few other ships equalled, let alone excelled, the reputation and achievements of the one-time flagship of the old Hutcheson fleet.

2
CHANCELLOR

The name *Chancellor* has been absent from the Clyde for nearly eighty years but in Victorian days, through long usage, it had become identified with steamers on the Arrochar route. Since practically the dawn of Clyde steamboat history there had been a service to the little village nestling amongst the hills at the head of Loch Long, its importance derived principally from through connections to Loch Lomond, then, as in later years, a tourist district of major importance. The circular tour embracing the 'Queen of Scottish Lakes' as well as the remote and beautiful Loch Long was one of the most popular day trips available to Victorian tourists, and for many years traffic was sufficiently profitable to justify double journeys daily during the summer months and the provision of excursion steamers of a class much superior to the usual standard of contemporary Clyde ships.

The Loch Long Station

The Dumbarton Steamboat Company was early in the field of Clyde passenger services, the distinctive black and white funnels of its quaintly old-fashioned steamers being a familiar sight for many years. With these owners originated the names *Premier* (1846) and *Chancellor* (1853), and the latter name became so closely associated with the Loch Long station that it was appropriated by successors, the Lochlong & Lochlomond Steamboat Company, when the original users went out of business. This second ship of the name entered service in 1864, placed on the route by the Lochlomond Company to secure a connecting service of prime importance to its own interests. That vessel occupied the station successfully for sixteen seasons, but towards the close of the 1870s there arose a need for a more modern steamer, the subject of this chapter.

The Lochlomond Company's minutes for 11 December 1879

recorded that the Dumbarton engineering firm of Matthew Paul & Co had agreed to build a steel paddle steamer to specifications and plans submitted for the sum of £7,900, an incredibly modest sum by modern standards, even allowing for the change in monetary values since those days. In accordance with common Clyde practice the engineering firm reserved for themselves the manufacture of machinery for the new steamer, sub-contracting building of the vessel herself to a local builder, Robert Chambers Jr of the Lower Woodyard, and hereby hangs the following fascinating and generally unknown story.

In later years Dumbarton shipbuilding and the justly famous Denny company became virtually synonymous, but during the second half of the nineteenth century several firms carried on business, with varying degrees of success, on the banks of the river Leven. One of these, the luckless partnership of Scott & Linton, is remembered today solely by the name of its most famous production, the majestic tea clipper *Cutty Sark*, now preserved at Greenwich. Even before completion of that lovely ship her builders had suspended payment, and she was completed by the neighbouring Denny firm, while the yard from which she had been launched in 1869 was leased to successive proprietors. So it was that Robert Chambers took over the Lower Woodyard in 1879 and there, in the following year, laid down a new *Chancellor* in the same cradle as the great clipper ship whose name is a household word to this day. Poor Chambers! The Lower Woodyard was unlucky for all its owners and he himself was forced to suspend payment in June 1881, having launched only eleven ships, including the *Chancellor*, his solitary venture into Clyde passenger service. It is quite possible that the new Arrochar steamer contributed to his failure, which he attributed to trade losses. As a new builder, anxious to establish a reputation for good value and so attract fresh orders, he probably tendered on the basis of minimal profit margins and was consequently unable to weather the shipbuilding trade depression of 1880 which affected Dumbarton very severely.

Tourist Comfort

The new *Chancellor* was only the second regular Clyde steamer to be built of steel, excepting the *Windsor Castle* of 1859, a largely experimental vessel which plied for but a single season. The first of the modern steel ships was David MacBrayne's *Columba*, built in 1878. Although of modest dimensions, the *Chancellor* was one of the neatest vessels of her class. There were saloons fore and aft, with alleyways round them on the main deck, an old-fashioned feature abandoned for Clyde vessels afterwards save only for the fitting of narrow fore-saloons to North British steamers as late as 1898. Loch Lomond steamers, however, continued to be built with narrow saloons fore and aft until the arrival of the *Empress*, the final example of this form of construction, in 1888. The *Chancellor* became, in fact, a prototype for subsequent Loch Lomond boats, with which she had many features in common. Accommodation on board all these steamers was markedly superior to that of the average 'doon the watter' boat sailing from Glasgow's Broomielaw to Rothesay, and the *Chancellor* herself had far better fittings than passengers expected to find in the vessels that carried city workpeople in their thousands to the coast each summer. 'The saloons and cabins are luxuriously appointed', ran an account in the *Lennox Herald*, 'and nothing that could be done for the comfort and convenience of the passengers has been neglected.'

The owners had funds to spare and they made the ship as comfortable and attractive as possible. To this end, comparatively expensive double diagonal machinery was installed, affording a smoother motion than the cheap and elementary single engines which propelled so many contemporary Clyde steamers. The double engine, with two high-pressure cylinders and twin cranks, avoided the wearisome surging of the single diagonal and was therefore preferred by the travelling public. Matthew Paul & Co provided the *Chancellor*'s steel haystack boiler as well as her machinery; working at a pressure of 50psi, it was 14ft in diameter, with a total heating surface of 2,600sq ft. The engineers evidently went to considerable lengths in making the engines; they were given an unusually good finish, to judge by newspaper reports, and it may be inferred that the working parts were machined bright in the manner common in later years.

The machinery was a success, besides being a finely finished job. The *Glasgow Herald* noted on the day of the *Chancellor*'s trials that 'it was a matter of general remark that the oscillation too often experienced on board river and other vessels was reduced to a minimum; in fact, the disagreeable sensation was only suggested to the steamer's passengers by its absence'. Enclosed by 'a very neat rail and wood balusters' the engines were fully open to view in what became the modern Clyde style. Earlier ships generally had their machinery shut away in an engine house to prevent the risk of being swamped by heavy seas breaking on board in the years when open foredecks were all but universal, and ventilation in the hot, enclosed space was poor. The arrangement in the *Chancellor* was therefore a great improvement.

The new steamer was launched from the Lower Woodyard on 21 April 1880 and 'as the vessel moved off the stocks towards the element which is to be the field of its future labours, it was, in good orthodox fashion, gracefully christened the 'Chancellor' by Mrs. Colonel Colquhoun, of Ben Cruach Lodge, Arrochar'. Fitting out was completed by the end of the following month and on 28 May the steamer went on trials. Leaving Helensburgh quay with a party of invited guests on board, she called at Greenock to embark more passengers and then proceeded to 'run the lights' – the traditional Clyde trial course of some sixteen miles between the Cloch and Cumbrae lighthouses – at an average speed of just over 14 knots. A newspaper report gave a much higher figure, quite improbable in the light of the vessel's subsequent history, and it seems clear that nautical miles had been confused with statute miles. Speed was never a major desideratum on the Arrochar station, and the *Chancellor*'s relatively modest prowess in this respect was realistic in view of the service for which she had been built. Having completed speed trials the steamer sailed into Loch Long and up to Arrochar where, in sheltered waters and to the music of the Bonhill Instrumental Band, the assembled company sat down to 'an excellent dinner, washed down by the waters of Epernay', thereafter going through the formal toast list inseparable from occasions of this kind. The guests returned to Helensburgh after six o'clock in the evening, doubtless very contented with a pleasant day's outing in the fine new steamer.

Practically the whole of the ship's covered accommodation for passengers was concentrated on the main deck, head room on the lower deck being inadequate for other than stores, crew's quarters and bars. The main dining room, following Loch Lomond practice, was in the forward saloon, in which 140 passengers could be served at one sitting. The fore end was reserved as a gentlemen's smoking room, separated by a partition from the dining section. Immediately aft of the engine room was to be found an unusual feature, a ladies' luncheon room 'handsomely fitted', together with another private cabin reserved for ladies. Abaft of these was the main first-class saloon which apparently could be utilised as a dining saloon if required, while at the stern was what was primly described as a 'commodious ladies' cabin, with lavatory'. The ship's galley was situated in a sponson house forward of the starboard paddle wheel, the corresponding position on the port side being occupied by a gentlemen's lavatory.

Early Service

The *Chancellor* finally left the builders' hands on 1 June 1880 to take up her station between Helensburgh and Arrochar under the command of Captain Alexander Neilson, senior master of the Lochlomond Company. Normally she lay overnight at Arrochar, departing thence at 6.40 in the morning for Helensburgh to connect with the 8.55 train to Glasgow. Returning at 10.35am, she gave connections at Greenock for passengers from the city by the Caledonian and Glasgow & South Western coast routes and called at Dunoon, Kirn, Hunter's Quay and Blairmore on a slow run to Arrochar. Leaving the head of Loch Long for the second time at 12.30pm, she retraced her path by way of the same piers, arriving at Helensburgh in good time to take up the down evening sailing to Kilcreggan, Cove, Blairmore and Arrochar with passengers by the 4.50 train from Glasgow (Queen Street), reaching her destination well into the evening after a very long day by modern standards. What a picture is conjured up by the *Chancellor*'s long-forgotten timetable, of businessmen rising from their beds in the early hours to join the steamer at Arrochar, breakfasting on board as she sped down Loch Long, and travelling into Glasgow over the old Helensburgh railway.

The North British coastal service operated from Helensburgh Quay until the company's new railhead at Craigendoran, on the eastern side of the town, was opened for traffic in 1882, when the

Chancellor as well as the railway steamers made that pier her headquarters. The building of Craigendoran formed the major part of a general improvement of North British services which had been started in 1879 with the provision of new rolling stock for the Helensburgh expresses and construction, to the designs of Dugald Drummond, the locomotive superintendent, of three large and handsome engines for working these trains. Named *Helensburgh, Roseneath* and *Craigendoran*, these magnificent express tank locomotives were probably the most modern of their kind in Britain at the time of their construction. Superbly arrayed in the company's golden yellow livery they were impressive machines and, by appearance as well as performance, helped to win new traffic for the Helensburgh route.

The paddle box of the *Chancellor*

The North British coast service was colourful in those years and steamers sailing from Helensburgh were amongst the most attractively arrayed on the Clyde. Amongst even these ships, however, the *Chancellor* was remarkable for the beauty of her colour scheme. An old water-colour shows her with black hull and white deck saloons panelled in pale pink. The paddle boxes were also white, and the funnel red, with black top. In common with many other Clyde steamers of the time the underbody of the hull was painted with salmon-coloured anti-fouling composition to a few inches above the water line, while the upper part was relieved by two gilt lines running from bow to stern just below main-rail level, and there was gilded decoration at bow and stern. The whole scheme was tasteful and effective and, while being bright and cheerful, was not in any sense gaudy.

The Arrochar service was usually carried on without incident and newspaper references to the *Chancellor* in her early years were few. However, towards the end of August 1880 she was involved in an alarming contest with the Rothesay steamer *Marquis of Lorne*, an incident all too typical of the period when rules and regulations governing navigation of passenger steamers on the firth were interpreted less strictly than in later years. When approaching Prince's Pier, Greenock, on her inward afternoon sailing from Arrochar, the *Chancellor* was overtaken by the *Marquis of Lorne*, on her way up from Rothesay. Neither captain gave way as the two vessels sailed side by side for over a mile; the *Chancellor*, in the inshore position, was in some danger of running aground and great alarm was caused amongst her passengers who expected a collision at any moment. The Arrochar steamer had the right of way and Captain Neilson frequently blew the *Chancellor*'s whistle to warn her rival off, but to little avail except to alarm the passengers still further. As the two steamers arrived at Prince's Pier the Rothesay boat was at last slowed to allow her rival into the berth and no harm resulted, but the incident was deplored as an example of gratuitous recklessness, the *Lennox Herald* making the obvious comment that 'even rivalry to secure passengers at Prince's Pier cannot be pleaded as an excuse for such unseemly conduct, as the Chancellor proceeds from Greenock to Helensburgh, while the Marquis of Lorne was on her way to Glasgow'.

The *Chancellor* seldom strayed from her normal station, but before starting the 1884 season she undertook a rare excursion from Dumbarton to Arrochar for the benefit of inhabitants of the Vale of Leven. Dumbarton was then served by a relatively new pier extending from the castle rock out into the main channel of the Clyde, but it was not as conveniently situated as the Old Quay in the river Leven, although the latter had fallen largely out of use. Nevertheless, it was from the Old Quay that the *Chancellor* was advertised to sail on 17 May 1884 to Arrochar and back on an afternoon excursion at the low fares of 1s for steerage passengers and 1s 6d for saloon accommodation. It was unfortunate that the response was poor, due to heavy rain which fell steadily until just before the time of sailing at 2.40pm, but the 400 passengers who did turn out enjoyed a pleasant excursion in sunshine and returned to Dumbarton at 8.30 in the evening where, noted a local reporter, 'the Quay presented a more animated appearance than it has done for a long time'.

New Owners

Following the building of the *Chancellor*, the Lochlomond Company was necessarily indebted to its bankers and, although profits were satisfactory enough to allow payment of an annual dividend, the remaining surplus was inadequate to allow rapid repayment of the overdraft. Nor did the construction of *The Queen* for the Loch Lomond service proper, in 1883, do anything to alleviate the situation. By the end of the following year the sum due to the bank was nearly £8,500 and annual interest of £440 had been incurred, an amount equal to nearly half of the dividend. Evidently the directors took fright and concluded that the company could no longer afford to maintain a steamer on the Arrochar route. Negotiations were therefore entered into with the Lochgoil & Lochlong Steamboat Company whose long connection with the Glasgow and Lochgoil trade made it a natural purchaser and, in March 1885, it was announced that the *Chancellor*, together with the goodwill of the Arrochar service, had been disposed of for the sum of £8,500, guarantees being given as to the safeguarding of the all-important Clyde section of the Loch Lomond and Loch Long circular tour.

The *Chancellor* was given a thorough overhaul, including the provision of a slightly larger funnel, and repainted in Lochgoil Company colours before returning to service under the flag of her new owners in May 1885. The very attractive Lochgoil funnel – red, with thin black and white bands separating the red from the black top – was of course adopted, and the saloon panelling modified; but uniquely in the Lochgoil fleet the steamer continued to sport white paddle boxes. Thus garbed, the *Chancellor* continued very much as before, sailing between Arrochar and Craigendoran under command of Captain Archibald Muir; but there were now appearances on excursion work, up river to Glasgow and elsewhere on the firth, usually relieving at times of holiday pressure. An unusual event was her charter, along with her consort *Edinburgh Castle* and the *Lord of the Isles* of the closely associated Glasgow & Inveraray

31

Steamboat Company, by the Dumbarton Equitable Co-operative Society on 15 May 1886 for a cruise from Dumbarton and Greenock to the Kyles of Bute to celebrate the society's silver jubilee, four thousand passengers being carried by the three vessels on that occasion.

Railway Service

If the purchase of the *Chancellor* by the Lochgoil Company was a logical change of ownership, her acquisition only a few years later by the Glasgow & South Western Railway was quite unexpected. A decision to operate a steamboat service on the Clyde was really forced upon the directors of that company by the loss of a significant proportion of its coast traffic to the Caledonian Railway following the opening of Gourock Pier in May 1889, a process disastrously accelerated when a competitive thrust was directed to Ardrossan and the Arran traffic, hitherto a South Western preserve, in 1890. By running a fleet of fast, modern paddle steamers through the transparent subterfuge of a closely associated Steam Packet Company, the Caledonian had been able to avoid parliamentary restrictions and appeared likely to command a virtual monopoly of the coastal traffic. This the Glasgow & South Western directors were determined to prevent. During 1890 their own steamboat connections from Prince's Pier and Ardrossan continued to be maintained by private owners under direct subsidy while Robert Morton, a distinguished marine consultant and naval architect, was commissioned to report on the question of the South Western running its own fleet of steamers. A bill was drafted, submitted to Parliament in the spring of 1891, and passed in midsummer. In normal circumstances it would probably have been thrown out, but much sympathy was shown to the company in its predicament and in the event powers were granted to operate steamers, with certain limitations intended to safeguard the legitimate interests of private owners.

In anticipation of receiving the necessary powers, the railway company approached various steamboat proprietors early in 1891 with offers to acquire their ships as soon as the bill became law. Amongst these was the Lochgoil Company which, in July, disposed of the *Chancellor* for £6,500, leaving the North British

Steam Packet Company to provide a railway connection to Loch Long from then on with the new *Lady Rowena*. Unlike most of the other tonnage bought at this stage, which was merely of a stopgap nature pending the building of new ships, the *Chancellor* was well suited to modernisation and a relatively long career in the Glasgow & South Western fleet. She was due for reboilering, and alternative tenders were invited for carrying out the work and installing a surface condenser, or converting the vessel to compound propulsion as well, based on specifications by Robert Morton. The Port Glasgow firm of Blackwood & Gordon was ultimately awarded the contract for reboilering and compounding the ship at a cost of £5,147, these alterations being carried out during the winter of 1891–2. In cases of conversion of Clyde steamers from simple to compound expansion it is sometimes difficult to know whether a new engine was installed or if the existing one was reconstructed. An entirely new cylinder and valve-chest casting would certainly have been required in the *Chancellor*, but existing components such as entablatures, crankshaft, connecting rods and valve gear might well have been used again, with modifications as required. The new boiler was of the marine, or navy, type working at a pressure of 125psi. Alterations were made to the hull to improve the *Chancellor*'s speed, and the passenger accommodation was remodelled and modernised.

Thus rejuvenated, the vessel ran trials on 14 April 1892, 'running the lights' at an average speed of 15 knots, being about $\frac{3}{4}$ knot faster than her previous record. She was no greyhound, but the South Western directors were well satisfied with their smart little steamer, which was placed on the Prince's Pier and Lochgoilhead station, varying her programme occasionally with spells on the Holy Loch route.

If anything, the radical modernisation of the ship had improved her appearance; a well-proportioned new funnel had been fitted and the fussy sponson houses of the original design replaced by new ones of improved type, although the distinctive paddle boxes remained unaltered. In the superb colours of the Glasgow & South Western fleet the *Chancellor* might well be thought to have been the daintiest, most attractive vessel of her class on the firth. The hull was painted dove-grey above a pink underbody; saloons, sponson houses and paddle boxes were white; and the funnel scarlet, with black top. At once striking and tasteful, it was a livery that enhanced any steamer to which it was applied.

The *Chancellor*'s career with her new owners was largely uneventful, although the railway company's records refer to a series of accidents to the paddle wheels, including breakages of driving rods, radius rods and paddle-wheel strengthening ring. The incidents tend to support the view that the ship's original wheels had survived her reconstruction and by the middle nineties were becoming subject to metal fatigue, but the paddle wheel is notoriously a weak point in a vessel of this type and we need not perhaps read undue significance into such incidents.

Sold Foreign

The *Chancellor*'s service with the Glasgow & South Western Railway lasted for ten years. By the turn of the century, however, she was one of only two survivors of the second-hand steamers which the railway company had acquired in the early nineties. In comparison with the splendid new vessels built for the Prince's Pier fleet her accommodation was dated and inadequate and the cost of improving her could not be justified, but her modern boiler and engine still made her an attractive bargain. Early in 1901, therefore, she was 'sold foreign' for the sum of £7,000 to La Herculina Ferrolana, a company operating services across the Bay of Corunna in north-west Spain, and there plied for a number of years under the name *Commercio* before ending her career as a barge.

There is a personal footnote to the story of this interesting little paddle steamer. In the years before World War I, the author's grandfather, along with several other British shipyard managers, took up a post in the naval shipyard at Ferrol, which is close to Corunna. It is inconceivable that the emigrants did not sail in the *Commercio* on occasions, and one wonders if they recognized in her an old Clyde favourite – a ship which they had known in earlier years in different guise. It was a strange combination of circumstances which had brought ship and men alike to the remote province of Galicia and, as far as the old *Chancellor* was concerned, an appropriately unusual conclusion to the little known story of her career.

3
MEG MERRILIES

If the first two steamers described in this book were outstandingly successful members of the Clyde excursion fleet, it would take a good deal of imagination to apply a similar description to the unlucky ship which was launched as the *Meg Merrilies* for the North British Steam Packet Company in 1883. During a relatively short career in home waters she was altered and re-altered, reconstructed and reboilered, and experimented upon at considerable cost, all to improve a vessel which was fundamentally of unsatisfactory design and never came up to expectations. Rejected by her first owners, sent to Ireland to retrieve her reputation, a cause of endless expense to her later Clyde owners, slow, and usually 'shy for steam', she departed for Rio after twenty years of misfortune, unwept and unlamented. Nevertheless, few Clyde steamers had such an unusual career, and the history of the *Meg Merrilies* well repays close study.

Craigendoran Flagship

When a series of major amalgamations in the middle of the nineteenth century gave a much enlarged North British Railway access to the Clyde coast at Helensburgh, plans were soon made to enter the excursion steamboat trade on the firth. Certain officers and directors formed an associated concern, the North British Steam Packet Company, under whose aegis an ambitious programme of sailings to Ardrishaig was inaugurated from Helensburgh Quay in 1866 with two large new saloon paddle steamers. Intended to capture a large share of the lucrative West Highland traffic from the Hutcheson fleet, the railway venture was dogged by misfortune – one of the steamers broke down early in the season, and after a few months the entire service was drastically curtailed when the railway company fell into serious financial difficulties. Having disposed of one of the steamers, the

Steam Packet Company was thereafter content to maintain a service to Dunoon and the Holy Loch which, if less spectacular than the brave project of 1866, nevertheless was a more soundly based commercial proposition and enjoyed reasonable success for the ensuing fifteen years.

In 1882 a reinvigorated and expanding North British Company re-entered the wider field of Clyde steamer services, opening a station and pier at Craigendoran, situated on a new loop line about a mile to the east of the terminus at Helensburgh. To revive the Rothesay service, abandoned ignominiously in the sixties, the company bought in the fast steamer *Sheila* from the Wemyss Bay fleet of Captain Alexander Campbell, and throughout the 1882 season that vessel maintained sailings from the partially completed Craigendoran pier. The service was an interim measure however until new steamers were built and the headquarters fully in operation, and the company went to Barclay, Curle & Co of Whiteinch for a new saloon steamer as its flagship in time for the opening of the 1883 summer season.

The new vessel was to be something rather special by Clyde standards. She was to be fast; and double diagonal, simple expansion machinery was provided to give extra speed. More power needed more steam; and two haystack boilers were required to supply the engines. So the design took shape – a long, slim hull with full width saloon aft, large paddle boxes with a handsome array of radial vents, and two smartly raked funnels placed forward of the paddles. The technical press duly reported her launch on 21 April 1883:

> As she left the ways, she was named the *Meg Merrilies* by Mrs Darling, wife of the secretary of the North British Steam Packet Company . . . After being canted in the river she was towed up to Finnieston, where she will receive her engines from the marine engineering establishment of the same firm . . . Steam is supplied by two boilers of improved construction, and she is expected to be propelled at a high rate of speed – the paddle floats being relatively large and powerful.

In her original condition the *Meg Merrilies* was not really a beauty, although in the new North British colours adopted for the opening of the full Craigendoran service she was undoubtedly striking. Her funnels were red, with broad white band and black top; the hull and paddle boxes black, with a profusion of gilding; and the saloon creamy white. The new flagship revived the name of one of the pioneer vessels of 1866, taken from the gypsy in Sir Walter Scott's well known novel *Guy Mannering*. The *Sheila* was renamed *Guy Mannering* at this time and she and the *Meg Merrilies*, along with the *Dandie Dinmont* of 1866, formed a trio of characters from this single novel.

The *Meg Merrilies* had her preliminary steam trials on 19 May and attracted much attention as she went down the river; but it was significant, in the light of after events, that 'the generally expressed opinion [was] that ... she appeared to sit somewhat low in the water'. None the less, all seemed well when she ran her official trials on 29 May and it was reported by the *Glasgow Herald* that 'the weather was very rough, the wind at times blowing almost half a gale, but notwithstanding this, a mean speed was obtained equal to 17 knots, or $19\frac{1}{2}$ statute miles per hour. The vessel behaved admirably'. The internal furnishings of the new steamer were much admired by the party of invited guests, the reporter noting that

> ... the saloon is very spacious, extending over the whole width of the vessel, and having an extreme length of 60 feet. At the entrance of the main saloon there is a smaller one for ladies. Both apartments are very nicely upholstered and decorated, and have a very handsome appearance. Behind the saloon – at the stern of the vessel – there is a space of about 10 feet, which, although left open at the back and sides, is covered over, and is intended to serve the purposes of a smoking room ... A dining saloon is fitted up in the fore part of the vessel ... Internally she has been luxuriously furnished with every modern requisite for securing the maximum amount of comfort for the travelling public.

The passenger accommodation of the *Meg Merrilies* thus left nothing to be desired and it was understandably with high expectations that Captain John McKinlay opened the Craigendoran service with his fine new steamer at the beginning of June, her consort on the Rothesay service being the erstwhile *Sheila*. From the outset, however, the *Meg Merrilies* was seen to be in trouble. The *Sheila*, six years her senior and inferior in passenger standards, could outsail her new sister with ease and, despite the official claim made for the latter at her trials, it is doubtful if the unfortunate *Meg Merrilies* could attain anything much in excess of 15 knots. She simply wallowed down the firth, looking exactly what she was – overloaded, and down by the stern. To add to her problems she suffered from steaming troubles and readily 'ran out of breath' when pressed to her maximum speed. She was probably too lightly built for her powerful and heavy machinery installation, a view supported not only by the dramatic improvement in performance following a later rebuilding but also by similar examples in other Clyde fleets. The gross over-powering of the *Eagle* of 1864 was a close parallel, and in that instance also a marked advantage resulted from the substitution of lighter engines and boilers.

Whatever the reasons the North British vessel was, all in all, a failure in terms of the expectations entertained of her when she entered service, and at the end of the year she was rejected by the Steam Packet Company and returned to her builders as unsatisfactory. It is likely that the owners had demanded too much and that in an attempt to incorporate all their requirements Barclay, Curle & Co had given themselves an impossible task. It is significant that when a replacement was ordered for the *Meg Merrilies* in 1884, the design was left entirely to the shipbuilders, save for the broadest outlines, and the Whiteinch yard redeemed its failure by producing the brilliant *Jeanie Deans*, whose prowess soon eradicated the unhappy memories of her ill-starred predecessor.

Campbell Interlude

With the *Meg Merrilies* thrown back on their hands, Barclay, Curle & Co decided upon drastic alterations. The underbody aft was reconstructed and the unusual extension of the promenade deck over the stern cut away with the object of lightening the ship, while the paddle wheels were modified in an attempt to improve her speed. Thus altered, the *Meg Merrilies* was chartered for a season to Belfast Lough where her failings were unknown and where doubtless her fine passenger facilities were much appreciated by passengers to Bangor.

She returned to the Clyde in 1885 under the flag of the respected and popular Captain Bob Campbell, whose white funnel fleet on the Glasgow and Kilmun station had been an institution for many years. Campbell's affairs underwent sharp fluctuations about this period; his trading partnership with Hugh Keith, of the Gareloch steamers, ran into financial difficulties and all their ships, including Campbell's flagship *Benmore*, had to be sold to Captain William Buchanan to settle debts. Only the timely and generous assistance of an influential group of friends who advanced enough money to purchase the *Meg Merrilies* saved him from his predicament and allowed him to resume business.

The new flagship was well suited for the Kilmun trade where lack of speed was not a disadvantage, and her comfortable saloon and smooth running machinery made her an immediate favourite. Consideration was given to renaming her *Blairmore* but happily the original name was retained. One detects perhaps a yearning on Bob Campbell's part for his old command, the *Benmore*, but that vessel, still in her old colours, was sailing to the Holy Loch in direct opposition to him in 1885. There had been recrimination between Buchanan and Campbell over the terms of sale of the old Kilmun fleet, Buchanan claiming that he had purchased not only the steamers but also the trade connection, while for his part Campbell maintained that he had always made it plain that he intended to resume a service at the first opportunity. Advertisement and counter-advertisement appeared in the *Glasgow Herald* in which the respective cases were stated at some length. It is likely that Buchanan, believing Campbell's affairs to be beyond recovery, felt it unnecessary to press him and that he failed to insist upon protective conditions in the sale agreement. Whatever the truth of the matter, rivalry flared during the summer of 1885 and the *Meg Merrilies* and the *Benmore* sailed at identical times for the coast. Although fares on the latter vessel were slightly cheaper, Bob Campbell's personal popularity and public sympathy for him eventually carried the day and the *Benmore* was withdrawn from the Holy Loch route at the end of the season.

Meanwhile, a consort for the *Meg Merrilies* had been delivered from McKnight & Co of Ayr, during the same summer. The new ship, the *Waverley*, was a fine, large saloon steamer rather in the style of the *Meg* but equipped with only one boiler and a single engine, and she was much faster than her sister.

Traffic continued to build up and Campbell went back to the Ayr yard in 1886 for the smaller *Madge Wildfire* for the Kilmun station, releasing the *Waverley* for a revived Glasgow–Ayr excursion service which had been in abeyance for several years. A single season saw this venture abandoned in favour of a profitable charter to Bristol, leaving the *Meg Merrilies* and the *Madge Wildfire* sailing as consorts to Kilmun.

Ill fortune continued to follow the *Meg*. In the winter of 1887 it is recorded that she suffered severe damage to one of her boilers and renewal became necessary. The opportunity was taken of substituting a single large haystack boiler – at 15ft high, 15ft diameter and working pressure of 50psi, said to be one of the largest yet built – for the two originally fitted and the steamer sailed thereafter with only one funnel, a change which improved her outline. In an effort to deal with the steaming problem the closed stokehold system was adopted, with forced draught. About the passenger accommodation there had been few complaints, but the provision of a dining saloon on the lower deck aft brought the *Meg Merrilies* well up to the highest Clyde standards. One of the paradoxes of her chequered career was that, despite serious mechanical shortcomings, she remained very much a favourite with the travelling public in view of her excellent facilities and the smoothness of her machinery.

Towards the end of 1888 Captain Bob Campbell died in Glasgow and the Kilmun fleet was managed thenceforth by his sons, Peter and Alex, both of whom had grown up in the Clyde steamboat trade. Neither was destined to make much of a mark in that sphere, for the successful experience of the *Waverley* on the Bristol Channel had encouraged them to expand their business interests in the south. The impending completion by the Caledonian Railway of an extension to Gourock, together with a new railhead and steamer terminal, brought home to the brothers the vulnerability to railway competition of their Kilmun sailings and they wisely decided to sell the *Madge Wildfire* and *Meg Merrilies*, along with the goodwill of the Holy Loch connection, to the Caledonian on 1 January 1889, concentrating thereafter on the development of a highly profitable excursion trade from Bristol, South Wales, and ports on the south coast of England.

Railway Ownership

The *Meg Merrilies* was taken into the fleet of the Caledonian Steam Packet Company Ltd, at a valuation of £8,000. She was laid up for the winter at the time of the change of ownership and did not appear in service as a Caledonian steamer until April 1889, almost certainly the first ship to emerge in the attractive colours of the new owners. Captain James Williamson, the secretary and manager, chose a hull livery of dark blue over the sea-green underbody of the Campbell steamers, the two colours separated by broad white boot-topping; saloons and sponson houses were pale pink, with pale-blue panelling; and the paddle boxes were painted white. The funnel was navy yellow, a colour then rare on the firth, and the house flag – a yellow pennant with a red lion rampant – completed an outstandingly tasteful and striking colour scheme.

Under her new owners the *Meg Merrilies* was one of the hardest worked members of the fleet. Surviving records for the period from 1889 to 1892 show her to have been in service for an average of about 250 days annually, sailing 26,000 miles per annum. In 1890 and 1891 she worked a longer season than any other Caledonian steamer. By the autumn of 1892 her boiler was worn out and the arrangements for renewal raised the wider issue of whether or not she should be sold and replaced by a new vessel. The company had invested heavily in new tonnage during the previous three years, however, and this consideration, coupled with the fact that the *Meg Merrilies* was still quite a modern steamer, may well have influenced the directors in their decision to have her reboilered by Barclay, Curle & Co during the winter of 1892–3 at a cost of £1,490, a new haystack being installed. Mechanically, the vessel was by this time out of date by comparison with her Gourock consorts, for her old Kilmun partner, the *Madge Wildfire*, had been given a navy boiler and converted to compound expansion two years earlier, thus falling into line with the other Caledonian steamers.

The *Meg Merrilies* continued her career as a general purpose ship for another five years, but towards the end of 1896 her condition again gave cause for concern. She was by then even more outdated by current Clyde standards, the more so when compared with the latest Caledonian acquisition, the superb

Duchess of Rothesay. Consideration was given to a suggestion that the second-hand navy boilers from another steamer, the *Marchioness of Lorne*, be used as replacements for the haystack fitted in 1892, but in the event this was not done, the boilers in question being sold instead to the Caledonian Railway locomotive department at St Rollox works, Glasgow. Early in 1897, however, the *Meg Merrilies* was involved in a collision which could have had serious consequences, and required a further spell in the hands of the shipbuilders.

On 29 January, commanded by Captain Duncan Bell, she was on the afternoon sailing from Wemyss Bay to Largs and Millport. Steamers on this route followed the coast for some distance over a course much favoured for speed trials of new ships, and so it was that on this afternoon the torpedo-boat destroyer No 289, *Electra*, racing down 'the Skelmorlie mile', overtook the Caledonian steamer on the approach to Largs and collided violently with her, smashing the stern bulwarks, knocking in the after end of the saloon, and causing something of a panic amongst the passengers, several of whom had been thrown off their feet by the force of the impact. The destroyer was in no better case, her bow being stove in, the first bulkhead torn away and many plates smashed and buckled. The *Meg Merrilies* was thought to be foundering and Captain Bell promptly ran her into shallow water and lowered the boats, but happily the damage was seen to be wholly above the water line and she was able to complete the return trip to Millport before limping up river for repairs. The *Electra* was also able to make her way back without incident to her builders at Clydebank. Captain Bell was an experienced skipper, known as a hard driver when circumstances warranted, and it was not his first experience of accident at sea. Many years before, when in command of the Wemyss Bay steamer *Sheila*, he had met the MacBrayne flagship *Columba* in a spectacular collision at Innellan and his vessel had had to be run aground to save her from sinking. Now his luck had run out. On 2 February 1897 the minutes of the Caledonian Steam Packet Company recorded laconically that 'Captain Bell's letter of resignation was submitted and accepted & in respect of his previous good conduct, it was agreed to give him three months' wages'.

The *Meg Merrilies* was repaired by A. & J. Inglis at the heavy cost of £1,400 and it is to be presumed that the work included overhaul of the boiler as well as reconstruction of the damage caused by HMS *Electra*. That the worn out haystack was far from being in satisfactory condition even then was evidenced by the fact that the ship was only granted a six months' passenger certificate from June 1897, under certain conditions laid down by the Board of Trade, and it was clear that the question of her future in the company's fleet was in the balance.

The Haythorn Episode

During the 1890s the marine water-tube boiler had been tried out in several forms in ships of the Royal Navy, and much interest was shown towards its application to commercial shipping. During the summer of 1897 the Caledonian manager, James Williamson, was approached by a Glasgow company, the Haythorn Tubulous Boiler Syndicate Limited, with a proposal that their water-tube boiler be tested in one of the Clyde steamers. Always keenly interested in engineering progress and alive to the possibility of improving the performance of a disappointing vessel, Williamson was eager to grasp the opportunity of trying out a novel form of boiler and at the same time cure the *Meg Merrilies* of her steaming troubles once and for all. Under certain guarantees and legal safeguards the steamer was therefore fitted with two Haythorn water-tube boilers, made by G. Inglis & Co Ltd of Airdrie, during the early months of 1898. They were installed by A. & J. Inglis at Pointhouse, where the *Meg Merrilies* was also converted to compound expansion by substitution of a 24in high-pressure cylinder for one of the original ones of 42in diameter, thus allowing maximum advantage to be taken of the new high-pressure boilers. These were designed to work at a pressure of 200psi, reduced to 130psi at the engine, and this arrangement necessitated the provision of a second waste steam pipe in front of the funnel, one of the few external signs of the radical alterations.

The Board of Trade insisted that for 'novel forms' of boiler only temporary passenger certificates would be granted, renewable at intervals of three months, and on this basis the *Meg Merrilies* re-entered service. The results of the reboilering were

43

nothing short of astonishing. A substantial improvement in buoyancy – she drew 7in less than before – allowed her to steam at least a knot faster and confirmed that her original boilers and machinery had been far too heavy for the relatively light hull. The Haythorn boilers steamed exuberantly and in combination with the newly compounded engine gave a dramatic reduction of no less than 50 per cent in coal consumption. A special trip was run on 28 April 1898, attended by representatives from the Admiralty and Board of Trade as well as other important guests. It seemed that the ship's problems had been solved at last and in an after dinner speech Captain James Williamson was understandably enthusiastic about the water-tube boilers which, he hoped, would be used in conjunction with triple expansion engines in the company's next steamer. Certainly the performance of the *Meg Merrilies* had been revolutionised and, with a sprightliness hitherto untypical of her work, she was placed on the Glasgow–Kilmun route which the Steam Packet Company still maintained as a legacy of the Campbell Holy Loch connection. Within a short period she was still further improved by the addition of a fore saloon which added considerably to her appearance. Meanwhile, in the same summer as the *Meg Merrilies* received her new boilers, in the south of England the Southampton, Isle of Wight & South of England Royal Mail Steam Packet Company purchased from John Gunn, of Cardiff, the Clyde-built paddle steamer *Lorna Doone*. Built by Napier, Shanks & Bell and engined by D. Rowan & Son in 1891 to the general specifications of Robert Morton, the *Lorna Doone* was a fine, handsome steamer; but in 1898 she was badly in need of repairs and a new boiler. The Southampton Company ran her for only one season before turning her over to J. Samuel White & Co Ltd of Cowes for reconstruction to the requirements of Mr C. W. Murray who, impressed by the success of the Haythorn installation aboard the *Meg Merrilies*, specified a more elaborate version for the *Lorna Doone*. That vessel accordingly emerged from White's yard in May 1899 with three improved water-tube boilers having uptakes into two funnels both placed forward of the paddles. The machinery, of compound diagonal pattern but in very poor order, was removed from the hull during alterations, then rebuilt with a new high pressure cylinder and completely re-erected before replacement in the *Lorna Doone*.

The renovated steamer went on trial on 20 May 1899, steaming just as freely as her Scottish cousin, and considered by everyone to be equally successful.

Back on the Clyde the Caledonian Steam Packet Company had arranged to pay the cost of the Haythorn boilers (£500) provided that the money would be refunded if the latter had to be removed due to failure within two years of November 1898. At some time in the summer of 1899, however, trouble was experienced with the water-tube installation; a minute in November refers to repairs and a demand for the Haythorn Syndicate's guarantee to be extended, failing which an offer by A. & J. Inglis to provide a new boiler of conventional design for £1,230 was to be accepted. Evidently there was dissatisfaction with the water-tube system after initial enthusiasm, and it is perhaps significant that in placing the order for their magnificent paddle steamer *Balmoral* with Hutson & Co of Glasgow in October 1899, the Southampton owners specified an improved haystack boiler instead of the Haythorn type. It is possible that disenchantment with the latter was in evidence even then, despite the apparent success of the *Lorna Doone*.

In January 1900 the Caledonian minutes recorded agreement to repairs costing £274 from which it may be inferred that the Haythorn Syndicate had agreed to extend their guarantee period, but the next official reference, late in February, told of the sudden end to the whole venture. While lying at Gourock on the morning of 29 January 1900 the *Meg Merrilies* was shaken by an explosion in the boiler room, caused by a bursting tube. Not only was the boiler itself damaged but so also was the hull plating, and several saloon windows were broken. In the flood of scalding steam and hot ashes which swept the stokehold one of the firemen, an Irishman named Patrick May, was so badly burned that he succumbed to his injuries in Greenock Infirmary on the following day.

The crippled steamer had to be towed to Greenock for repairs, and dry dock survey revealed hull damage which cost £120 to make good. James Williamson had had enough of the Haythorn boilers and at once instructed their replacement by a single new boiler of the standard navy type, installed by A. & J. Inglis under their offer of the previous autumn. The Haythorn experiment, begun with such high hopes, ended in legal action by the

Caledonian Steam Packet Company to recover the cost of repairs and alterations made necessary by the accident and subsequent reboilering, and the last we hear of the Syndicate is of its formal winding up in 1901. So ended in failure what might otherwise have developed into an important Scottish engineering venture, and one can only regret that uncertainty with regard to the maintenance and operation of a novel form of steam generator frustrated James Williamson's bold attempt to advance steamship design.

Epilogue

Rebuilt to standard Caledonian requirements, the *Meg Merrilies* returned to service but her Clyde career was nearly done. She now presented her most attractive appearance, for the fore-saloon added at the time of the Haythorn installation survived the latter's removal. Gone at last was the gawky outline of the eighties, and in the smart colours of the Steam Packet Company the *Meg* was a neat, almost pretty, steamer. Her final reconstruction cannot have improved her speed, however, and it was plain that nothing further could reasonably be expected in that direction. The arrival of a new modern paddle steamer, the *Duchess of Montrose*, in the early summer of 1902 led to the disposal of the *Meg Merrilies*. An offer to purchase her was received from agents acting for the Leopoldina Railway Company of Brazil, and the ship changed hands in July of that year for £5,000. The Clyde Shipbuilding & Engineering Company prepared her for the Atlantic crossing, building a turtle deck over the exposed bow, boarding up the saloon windows and otherwise strengthening the hull and paddle boxes. In this unusual condition she finally sailed from Gourock at the end of August, laden with coal, and in due course safely rolled down to Rio where, for the next twenty years and rechristened *Maua*, she pursued a career as ferry across that beautiful bay, being eventually broken up in 1921.

It is doubtful if any other Clyde steamer had such a chequered history as this formerly well known and now all but forgotten ship. The cause of worry to practically everyone who ever had to deal with her, she suffered more mechanical and structural alterations than any of her contemporaries as successive efforts were made to improve a ship which must be classed as one of the Clyde's few failures. In spite of all her faults, however, the story of the *Meg Merrilies* contains more interest than that of many a more efficient vessel.

4

GRENADIER

During the 1870s the well known firm of J. & G. Thomson had moved down river from the old town of Govan to their new and better known Clydebank yard, and there in 1885 they built a new excursion paddle steamer to the order of David MacBrayne – one which stood out from her contemporaries as a supreme example of the art of naval architecture. The builders had turned out many beautiful ships but in this, the last of a famous series for the celebrated West Highland fleet, they surpassed themselves, producing a vessel which was widely acclaimed as one of the most attractive little steamers that ever graced Scottish waters.

Oban and the North

The West Highland town of Oban has long been an important tourist centre, being strategically placed to give access to the Firth of Lorne, the Isle of Mull and the southern Hebrides. Its modern development was given impetus by the opening of the Callander & Oban Railway in 1880, and its reputation rapidly became such as to justify the unfortunate but often quoted description, 'the Charing Cross of the Highlands'. Oban soon became the principal operating centre of the MacBrayne fleet, a position which it has largely maintained ever since. Perhaps the best known tour originating here was the day excursion round the Isle of Mull to Staffa, the little island of bizarre geological formation immortalised in Felix Mendelssohn's overture *The Hebrides*, and to Iona, the ancient seat of Scottish Christianity. On these peaceful and breathtakingly beautiful seas thousands have sought relaxation and enjoyment for over a century, and still continue to do so.

It is sixty years now however since another excursion, of still greater scenic grandeur, ceased to be operated out of Oban – a

The *Duchess of Fife* in her final condition, leaving Largs in the autumn of 1951. *Photograph by the Author*

The celebrated Hutcheson flagship *Iona* as sailing in the 1890s. She is seen here leaving Gourock Pier on her outward run to Ardrishaig. *John Crosby Collection*

The Dumbarton-built paddle steamer *Chancellor*, as sailing for the Lochgoil & Lochlong Steamboat Company from 1885 to 1891. *G. E. Langmuir Collection*

The unlucky *Meg Merrilies*, seen in Rothesay Bay during the early 1890s. A fore saloon was added at a later date. *G. E. Langmuir Collection*

tour which beyond question was the finest of its kind in the British Isles. This holiday route from the shores of Lorne to Gairloch in Wester Ross traversed the loveliest and most dramatic scenery in all Scotland, passing as it did through the Sound of Mull, rounding the westernmost mainland point of Britain at Ardnamurchan and continuing on past the Small Isles to the Sound of Sleat and Loch Alsh, the outlook to the west dominated by the mountains of Skye as the steamer sailed north to its lonely destination. The old steamer *Mary Jane*, much modernised, improved and renamed *Glencoe*, was placed on the then new route in 1875 and included calls at Loch Scavaig and Portree in those day-long voyages. In time the majesty of the route itself and the provision of rail access to Oban led to an upsurge in traffic justifying the provision of a new steamer, and late in 1884 David MacBrayne – by then an active septuagenarian – went back to the shipbuilders who, over a period of thirty years, had produced for his former partners, the brothers Hutcheson, and himself such lovely and successful ships as the *Mountaineer*, the three *Ionas* and the majestic *Columba*. The new vessel, the builders' No 224 and their last paddle steamer for West Highland service, fittingly marked the peak of aesthetic development in this class of ship.

The intention was that she should undertake the Glasgow and Ardrishaig mail service during the winter months, and the all-the-year-round nature of her work goes some way towards explaining why she was fitted out with a most unusual pattern of machinery. Fuel economy was obviously essential, and a compound engine was therefore used for the first time in Clyde service. Nevertheless, the cost of coal was probably not the determining factor; almost certainly the object was to extend the vessel's range of sailing in a day's work, a matter of great importance on the long Gairloch route. Diagonal engines working on the compound principle were then in use elsewhere and it might have been expected that the MacBrayne steamer would be so equipped; but J. & G. Thomson chose to rely, as so often before, on the outmoded oscillating type, producing in this instance a rare, if not unique, compound version which was never repeated in this or any other Scottish fleet. Although old-fashioned, the oscillating engine had the useful advantage of being almost free of the rhythmic surging associated principally with the popular and widely used single diagonal engine, and never quite absent from twin crank diagonal machinery. An oscillating engine's cylinders were placed under the crankshaft and because the connecting rods drove upwards on to it the usual thrusts and forces were vertical, and did not affect the motion of the ship. In a tourist vessel intended for one of the best known MacBrayne services, this consideration may well have influenced the decision to perpetuate, albeit in modernised form, a style of propulsion which had been in its heyday thirty years earlier.

The steamer was beautifully designed, with a long, raking hull, a fiddle bow and counter stern. She was modelled on the National Line's *America*, turned out by the same yard in the previous year, and was really a miniature version adapted for paddle propulsion. There were deck saloons fore and aft, extending to the full width of the hull. They could perhaps have been longer, but their proportions were perfect. The external appearance was enhanced by the use of wide observation windows which were in pleasing contrast to the contemporary narrow, vertical ones in saloon steamers of other fleets. Paddle boxes of standard MacBrayne pattern were used, with seven fan vents and the usual elaborate gilding. The only features which could be faulted aesthetically were the design and positioning of the ship's two funnels, which were rather slim and placed close together fore and aft of the paddle boxes, resulting from the use of navy boilers which were notoriously awkward to place in a steamer's hull without disturbing the profile.

In spite of this, however, the new vessel was unusually handsome and regarded as one of the beauties of her time. A feature of the original design, abandoned during building, was a mainmast; but such a provision in a ship of her type might well have marred the steamer's appearance. Howden's system of forced draught was installed at a cost of £275, evidently as a modification of the original specification, and amongst other up to date items she was equipped with a surface condenser, steam windlasses and Muir & Caldwell's steam steering gear. Building costs were recorded as £7,676 for the hull, £5,128 for machinery and £2,074 for boilers which, after allowance for sundry items, gave J. & G. Thomson a profit of £830 out of the contract price of £15,900.

Early Days

The steamer was launched on 19 March 1885 by her owner's niece, Miss Brown, of Claremont Gardens, Glasgow, who named her *Grenadier* – the first of a series of ships given military titles at that period, perhaps inspired by David MacBrayne's connection with the Volunteers. Whatever may have been thought of the propriety of such a name, it was a gift to the Glasgow wits, who bestowed upon the vessel the affectionate soubriquet of 'Grannie Dear'. In retrospect, one regrets the failure to confer upon such an attractive ship one of the lovely Gaelic names which would have been so much more in keeping with her sphere of activity. She ran a trial trip on the Clyde on 14 May, carrying on board David MacBrayne and a small party of his invited guests. On the measured mile at Skelmorlie, her engines working at 42rpm, the *Grenadier* achieved a speed of 16 knots – no great rate by the highest standards of the time, but perfectly adequate for her specialised duties which demanded economy first. That she was able to maintain a consistent speed was amply proved on a long run through Rothesay Bay and round the island of Bute before returning to port. Her passengers were favourably impressed with the new boat, the correspondent of the *Glasgow Herald* being particularly struck by the light and airy saloons and dining accommodation on the lower deck aft. 'Internally the steamer is a model of economical and harmonious arrangement . . . and altogether . . . is one of the most comfortable which the most fastidious traveller need desire.'

The *Grenadier* spent her first weeks in service on the Ardrishaig mail run under the command of MacBrayne's senior master, Captain John McGaw, but the commissioning of the *Iona* in early June released her for the West Highland sailings and she made her first passage from Greenock round the Mull of Kintyre on 8 June 1885. The *Oban Times* reported that

> . . . this magnificent steamship arrived in Oban Bay on Monday night about 11 o'clock, signalising [sic] her arrival by a discharge of the cannon on board. She made the passage . . . in the hitherto unapproached time of 8 hours and 45 minutes. On Tuesday she was placed on the 'Royal Route' chain between Oban and Crinan, and during the week has made the runs in marvellously short time.

David MacBrayne's shipping agent at Oban in those days was Alexander Brown who, with an astute eye to business, invited a large number of the local merchants to enjoy an evening cruise in the Firth of Lorne during that first week in order to see for themselves the attractions of the splendid new paddle steamer. She appeared also on the Fort William service but when the *Iona* followed her to Oban later in the month, the *Grenadier* at last took up the Gairloch sailings. Little is recorded of her first season's activities, but the extent of her success may be gauged from a paragraph in the *Oban Times* during August, which noted that

> ... this magnificent steamer is making wonderful time on her runs from Oban to Gairloch, &c. She made the passage the other day in the shortest time on record. Besides being swift, she is a good sea boat. Both builders and owners are to be congratulated on the 'Grenadier'.

Not for the first time, David MacBrayne had got a bargain.

It appears that the *Grenadier* was transferred to the Oban and Iona service after only one year on the Gairloch route, for the local press reported her having been badly delayed by fog on her cruise round Mull on 1 July 1886. It is possible that traffic on the northern route had not developed as quickly as anticipated, and that the *Grenadier* proved to be too large a ship for the trade. The building of a similar, but smaller, steamer for the Gairloch run in 1888 perhaps supports this conjecture. At any rate, it is certain that by the end of the eighties the *Grenadier* had settled firmly into the pattern which, with few breaks, she was to follow for the rest of her career on the west coast, that is to say, serving as Ardrishaig mail steamer during the winter and as the Iona excursion vessel in the summer months.

An official guide booklet published by David MacBrayne gives interesting details of the *Grenadier*'s summer programme during the early nineties, when she normally took up the Iona service in June and maintained it throughout July, August and September. In keeping with the religious principles of her owner, and equally in accord with the convictions of the local population, the ship never sailed on Sundays. Otherwise, her route alternated daily: on Mondays, Wednesdays and Fridays she sailed outwards by the Sound of Mull, and on the remaining days of the week by the south end of Mull. Departing at eight o'clock in the morning, the steamer allowed passengers an hour and a half ashore at Iona and a similar time at Staffa, returning to Oban at about half-past five in the afternoon. The main contrast with the service of modern times lay in the calls at several piers which are now either abandoned or are no longer served by the Iona steamer – at Carsaig, in Loch Buie, which has disappeared, Craignure and Salen, in Mull; and Lochaline, in Morven. For the round trip, exclusive of meals, the first-class fare was 15s including the services of guides and boatmen at Staffa and Iona. Charges for catering on board the *Grenadier* were certainly not excessive; for breakfast, dinner and tea (with meat) 'served in first-class style' a passenger paid only 2s or 3s for each meal.

Summer and Winter

Few experiences in Scottish tourism were as idyllic as the Iona excursion on board the *Grenadier*, embracing as it did the scenic glories of Morven and the Isle of Mull, the bizarre outlines of Staffa and the Treshnish Isles, and the crystalline waters of the Sound of Iona. On one of those heavenly days of clear visibility and strong sunshine which are far more common in the Hebrides than is often realised, the sight of the *Grenadier* riding at anchor off Martyrs' Bay must have been unforgettable, her beautiful lines and bright colours an ideal contrast to the soft blues of sea and sky. Such was the setting in which most people remembered her, but the Iona service was simply the high point of her year's work. Throughout the winter and spring the *Grenadier*'s duties consisted of the daily run from Glasgow or Greenock to Ardrishaig and back with the Royal mails in place of her larger sisters *Iona* and *Columba*, both of which were too large and uneconomical for the sparse off-season trade. Many people are surprised to learn that, in terms of annual sailing mileage, the *Grenadier* was really a Clyde steamer, a vessel which sailed with great regularity and reliability for many years on her owner's principal route.

The Firth of Clyde is generally more sheltered than the outer waters of the west coast of Scotland, but conditions in winter could be as dangerous as anywhere and the *Grenadier*'s timetable was now and again disrupted by storms or fog. The open stretch of lower Loch Fyne between Ardlamont Point and Kintyre was notoriously hazardous in stormy weather and even with the sturdy *Grenadier*'s saloon windows boarded up against rough seas there were occasions when her skippers wisely declined to face the exposed run across to Tarbert. The combination of bad weather and high tides sometimes made it impossible to make the usual calls, a typical occasion being 25 January 1890 when the highest tide recorded for six years flooded the piers at Innellan, Colintraive and Tighnabruaich, while the conditions at Ardlamont were described as 'fearful'. Even Dunoon and Rothesay piers were overwhelmed at times, causing interruption of the normal service. Fog, the other danger, as often as not brought river traffic to a standstill. Usually this occurred on the river and upper firth but less frequently, as on 6 February 1890, thick weather extended far down the coast, and the *Grenadier* had to tie up at Colintraive on her outward run and wait until it cleared.

Accidents

In the course of a long career it was inevitable that occasional mishaps should befall even such a well-run steamer, but no serious accident was ever attributable to her captain and crew. One afternoon in February 1887 the *Grenadier* was leaving Dunoon on the up run from Ardrishaig when the starboard paddle wheel struck a floating log, disabling her completely. She had to be towed to J. & G. Thomson's yard at Clydebank for repairs while her place was taken by another steamer for three days. That incident, although troublesome, caused no injury to passengers, but just over two years later the *Grenadier* was involved in one of the few fatal accidents to a Clyde steamer in normal service. She was returning to Greenock with a large complement of passengers and, on approaching Colintraive pier in the eastern Kyles of Bute, Captain Donald McCallum and his pilot, James Gillies, saw the coasting schooner *Lady Margaret* lying at the quay discharging lime. The sailing vessel hauled off to allow the mail steamer to take the pier, and Captain McCallum instructed Gillies to cut inside her to make the Colintraive call. Unfortunately, as he did so a gust of wind caught the schooner, swinging her stern into the *Grenadier*'s path. The engines were immediately reversed, but too late to prevent the steamer's starboard paddle wing catching the jibboom of the coaster and carrying away her mast. It fell across the *Grenadier*'s deck, striking a group of passengers, killing one instantly and severely injuring another.

The unexpected tragedy led to an official inquiry. McCallum and Gillies were arrested and examined before Sheriff Campion at Inveraray early in May, but it was clear that they had been powerless to avoid the accident. Both men were liberated on bail, and all proceedings were dropped by the procurator fiscal a few days later. It had been a sad and unusual accident involving one of the Clyde's most experienced skippers, but the rarity of such an occurrence emphasized the general immunity of the river fleet from major misfortune, then and in any subsequent period.

Reconstruction

By the turn of the century the *Grenadier*'s original boilers were due for replacement after sixteen years of continuous service and, as in the earlier example of the *Iona*, there was a reversion to the apparently outmoded haystack pattern when she was refitted in the winter of 1901–2. Technical improvements in design, largely due to the Kelvinhaugh firm of Hutson & Corbett, had given the old type of boiler a new lease of life however, and examples were successfully used not only in the modernisation of existing paddle steamers but also in several new ships at that time. In the case of the *Grenadier*'s conversion the alterations did not just improve her appearance, but transformed the vessel into one of the most outstandingly beautiful steamers of her class ever to sail in British coastal waters. The fitting of new funnels of larger diameter, placed further apart than the originals, balanced her outline to perfection and made the vessel a veritable swan amongst her contemporaries. Always an attractive ship, the *Grenadier* after reboilering was quite unusually graceful, and a classic example of how attention to detail can transform the appearance of a ship.

After alterations the *Grenadier* spent the summer of 1902 on the Clyde, providing an extra service from Rothesay to Glasgow every weekday, returning from the city at 1.30pm to Tighnabruaich, a service extended on Saturdays to a cruise round the island of Bute. This programme augmented the existing Ardrishaig service afforded by the *Iona* and *Columba*. It is difficult to understand why it was done, unless to take advantage of anticipated traffic following the Glasgow Exhibition year of 1901. Whatever the reason, the unusually lavish MacBrayne service was not repeated and the *Grenadier* returned to the Staffa and Iona run in 1903.

She remained on the Ardrishaig route in winter, alternating annually with the Oban summer season until the middle of World War I, by which time many excursion services had been given up due to lack of traffic and shortage of ships. Early in the war the Admiralty had found that shallow-draught paddle steamers were well suited for minesweeping, and consequently many peacetime pleasure vessels were requisitioned into naval service for this purpose. The harbours on the east coast of Britain were particularly vulnerable to minelaying by German submarines and most auxiliary vessels were based in the south and east coast areas. The MacBrayne fleet of the period contained few ships suitable for naval work, most being either too old or otherwise unfitted by their design for the duties involved. Many were therefore employed on Clyde routes during the wartime period to release more modern steamers for Admiralty service, but the *Grenadier* was eventually requisitioned in July 1916 to serve as a minesweeper. She worked in the North Sea as auxiliary vessel No 536, being temporarily renamed HMS *Grenade* to avoid confusion with an existing warship, and was discharged safely to return to her lawful peacetime occasions in October 1919. She was the only MacBrayne steamer used on active service.

How long this most attractive of paddle steamers might have continued to sail on the stations which she had made so much her own is a matter for conjecture. By the mid 1920s the MacBrayne company, hard hit by soaring fuel and wages costs after the war, was in no financial condition to modernise its fleet. Many of the ships maintaining essential Hebridean services all the year round were outdated in terms of speed and comfort. The *Grenadier*, merely a summer butterfly in these waters, was smartly turned out and well run, but she was over forty years old. It was no secret that matters would come to a head in 1928 when the company's mail contract was due for renegotiation and, in fact, it did not tender for a renewal. A radical reorganisation of fleet and services after control had passed out of Scottish hands in the thirties swept away much that was archaic, and it is unlikely that the *Grenadier* would have survived beyond the middle of that decade. As it happened however her end came quite unexpectedly and tragically, at the close of the Oban summer season of 1927.

Disaster

Captain Archibald Macarthur had commanded the *Grenadier* for many years and by all accounts had been loath to leave the ship on his retirement in 1926. Sensitive to the feelings of an old and trusted employee, the company made an arrangement under which Captain Macarthur sailed as additional master in 1927, officially to advise his successor, Captain MacLean, but to all intents and purposes virtually in his old command, and so matters ran throughout that season. At the beginning of September the *Grenadier* had almost completed her summer duties – one more trip to Iona would finish her spell at Oban – after which she was to sail back to the Clyde to resume the Ardrishaig mail service. Her usual overnight berth was at the North Pier and it was there, during the early hours of 6 September, that Oban's inhabitants were startled from their sleep by an unexpected commotion. To those who looked out, the sight which greeted them was horrifying – the *Grenadier* was a mass of flames. The outbreak had spread with frightening speed as possibly an accidentally dropped cigarette, or a galley fire, took the crew by surprise. The old steamer, built largely of wood and furnished with inflammable materials, caught alight like tinder. Most of the crew were roused in time to scramble ashore, but their personal effects had to be left on board the doomed vessel. These were the lucky ones. Three others, including Captain Macarthur, were trapped and died in the fire. From the first it was clear that the ship was beyond saving and all that could be done was to warp her away from the pier by means of a rope from the bow. The fire ran its course and the *Grenadier* eventually settled on the bed of the harbour, her saloons and funnels, charred and blackened, standing clear of the water as hideous reminders of the tragedy.

It was a sad end to a career which had hitherto been one of the happiest in the MacBrayne fleet. Many thousands of travellers who associated the old steamer with carefree trips to the Isle of Iona must have heard of her fate, and the deaths of her crew, with horror. There was a half-hearted attempt to see if the vessel could be repaired, but the cost of doing so was patently prohibitive. The wreck of the once beautiful paddle steamer was refloated during 1928 and left Oban Bay in May of that year under tow for Ardrossan, where she was broken up. Her haystack boilers were undamaged and were refitted, one each, to the veterans *Glencoe* and *Gondolier* of the same fleet.

It is nearly forty years now since the sound of paddle wheels was heard regularly in Oban Bay, and the Hutcheson and MacBrayne 'swift steamers' are only a fading memory. Nevertheless, when the gloaming is over Oban and the setting sun has left only a red glow over Kerrera, and the great hills of Mull stand out black against the twilight of a summer evening, fancy still suggests that at the North Pier, as in days long gone, there lies the trim shape of the beautiful little steamer *Grenadier*.

5

LUCY ASHTON

Some of the best known Clyde steamers were 'maids of all work' – vessels of intermediate size and power, combining economy of operation with sheer handiness. Ships of this type, lacking much of the glamour attaching to the large cruising steamers, were seldom recalled as first favourites by holiday visitors to the firth. Local residents, however, took a different view, for the smaller vessels, often sailing throughout the year in fair weather and foul, provided the backbone of the coast services with absolute reliability. In the late 1880s there was launched from the shipyard of T. B. Seath & Co, in the ancient and royal burgh of Rutherglen, a Clyde steamer in which these virtues were perhaps more happily combined than in any other and whose career was to span a period of no less than sixty years. The new ship was the much loved *Lucy Ashton*.

Early Years

We have already seen that the North British Steam Packet Company was the title of a partnership of certain directors and officers of the North British Railway, which was obliged to run its Clyde steamboat services under an independent arrangement in order to circumvent parliamentary prohibition on direct ownership of marine interests by railway companies. The 1880s saw a considerable expansion of the services from the new port at Craigendoran, and several new ships were added to the fleet to cater for traffic to Rothesay and the Gareloch. These vessels outclassed the company's remaining original steamer of 1866, the *Dandie Dinmont*, which was employed on the Holy Loch route, and towards the end of the decade it was decided to replace her by a new ship. On 24 May 1888 therefore Miss Darling, daughter of the company's secretary and manager, launched from Seath's yard the steel hull of the *Lucy Ashton*. In common with most Craigendoran steamers the new boat bore the name of a character in one of Sir Walter Scott's novels, in this instance the ill-fated heroine of *The Bride of Lammermoor*. The Rutherglen shipyard had built the steamer on a sub-contracting arrangement with their principals, Hutson & Corbett, engineers, of Kelvinhaugh, and accordingly the hull was towed down the river by teams of horses and men, across the weir at Glasgow Green, and down to the fitting-out basin, to have her boiler and machinery installed by the Glasgow firm.

In her original condition the *Lucy Ashton* was absolutely typical of her period and in all essentials, mechanical and thermal, differed little from the practice of the sixties and seventies. The major improvements in design lay in the use of steel instead of wrought iron for the low-pressure haystack boiler which, fired with great quantities of cheap coal, raised steam quickly and abundantly; and in the use of a surface condenser instead of one of the jet pattern. But the ship was driven by the well-tried single engine which combined cheapness with reliability and for these reasons had been widely favoured for over twenty years. There was a deck saloon aft, the full width of the hull; and a very small saloon, with alleyways round it, was placed on the main deck forward. The hurricane deck covering boiler and engine was extended fore and aft across the saloons to form a promenade deck. There was no navigating bridge as now understood, and the steersman (the 'pilot' on Clyde steamers) stood on a small raised platform on the promenade deck between the paddle boxes to work the large, wooden hand-steering wheel. Above him, abaft of the funnel, was a narrow bridge spanning the paddle boxes, with engine-room telegraphs to port and

The paddle box of the *Lucy Ashton*

starboard. Here stood the captain, ideally placed to give orders and guide the steamer into piers.

The *Lucy Ashton* was always a pretty little steamer but perhaps appeared at her best when new from her builders. The shapely hull was well complemented by the saloons and large paddle boxes with radial vents, while the funnel was symmetrical, well-placed, and smartly raked. The rich North British colour scheme of the eighties further enhanced her appearance. The hull was black, with pale-pink underbody carried slightly above the waterline, two relieving gilt lines were carried from stem to stern round hull and sponsons just below the level of the main rail while the paddle boxes, also black, were richly gilded and decorated. Saloons were cream with brown panelling, set off by white washboards at promenade-deck level and white lifeboats, one on each side of that deck, aft of the paddle boxes. The funnel was painted bright red, with a broad white band and black top. Two apparently trivial features contributed in their own way to the overall effect. The long, thin galley chimney, projecting from the promenade deck at the forward end of the port sponson repeated the funnel colours, but without a white band, while the stay ring between the red and white portions of the main funnel was painted black. This latter feature was never abandoned by the North British Steam Packet Company and its successors, and possibly was derived from the heraldic practice of dividing colours from each other by thin black fimbriations.

During her splendid career the *Lucy Ashton* was substantially renovated and reconstructed on more than one occasion, as well as receiving routine maintenance. In course of time therefore she acquired something of the character of the legendary Irishman's jack-knife, which had been given two or three new handles and blades, but was still regarded as being the original article. Consequently, the steamer so familiar to those who knew her in her later years would have appeared quite differently to those same people had they seen her when she first came down river in the summer of 1888. Examination of early photographs reveals an elegance and simplicity of design which was lost in the many improvements made later in the interests of comfort and safety. One is impressed by the clean lines of the hull and the well-proportioned deck saloons although, to be truthful, passenger accommodation was inclined to be austere, particularly in the steerage. The traveller of a later generation would have noted the absence of promenade-deck seats in the form of the, to him, familiar buoyant apparatus, the absence of life-saving gear apart from the two boats and a few lifebelts, and the use of wood for the forward bulwarks on the main deck. He would almost certainly have been impressed by the richness of livery and finish on this maid-of-all-work and by the standard of cleanliness of the vessel's decks and fittings, contrasting markedly with the prolific volumes of smoke pouring from the funnel. The *Lucy Ashton* was mechanically and thermally typical of her day and the haystack boiler, fired with cheap coal, raised steam quickly and abundantly only at the cost of heavy fuel consumption.

Communicating stairs between the promenade and main decks were situated on the sponsons in the early years and gave access to a small, enclosed engine room. This was a necessary precaution to prevent serious flooding in the event of heavy seas breaking in upon the sponsons' almost unprotected forward end, but in steamers of the *Lucy Ashton*'s type it prevented close examination of the machinery in the manner to which passengers became accustomed in later ships. Not that there was much to see, in any case, in the young *Lucy*. The single connecting rod and crank of the diagonal engine rose and fell, half hidden, between massive cast-iron entablatures bolted to the cylinder casting; auxiliary machinery was minimal, consisting of a condenser pump worked by arms from the crosshead, and a boiler feed pump. Controls were of the simplest, an elementary lever panel and damper control valve to the haystack boiler being adequate for all purposes. This engine room and, indeed, the entire vessel, was lighted by oil lamps which, if a good deal less efficient than electricity, nevertheless gave a pleasing mellow glow.

Such were the more important features of our Victorian paddle steamer – a trim, smart, little vessel rather strange to modern eyes in many respects but recognizably the basic North British steamer of the next forty years and more. The *Lucy Ashton*, in her original condition of the eighties, must have looked a perfect picture at Craigendoran alongside her North British consorts as well as the Loch Long steamer *Chancellor* and the famous 'teetotal' boat, the *Ivanhoe*, which also at that time made Craigendoran their headquarters. Picture her paddling purposefully down the Holy Loch with the grasshopper surging of her single engine on a summer morning of glassy calm, and you have some idea of the pleasure which she gave to so many travellers as she bore them away from the grime of Glasgow to the delectable holiday resorts of the Firth of Clyde.

Reconstruction

The first change in the *Lucy Ashton*'s appearance consisted of the addition of a purser's office in 1894, a new bridge being placed on top of this deckhouse. The new layout meant the transfer of the steering wheel to the bridge – a much improved and more sensible arrangement for navigating the ship. The position of the bridge itself is interesting. When the *Lucy Ashton* was new, the almost universal Clyde practice was to place it between the paddle boxes, so that on a conventional single-funnelled vessel it was abaft of the funnel. On the small steamers of that period the lookout ahead was not too seriously impaired by the funnel and, as we have noted, the captain had the considerable advantage of direct access to the paddle boxes, which was a much more important consideration in a ship calling frequently at piers. Only with the introduction of larger steamers in the nineties, and partly at least as a result of a series of collisions with small craft, did the practice begin to change; the Caledonian Steam Packet Company rapidly adopted the modern position forward of the funnel, followed in time by other owners, but many preferred the time-honoured position between the paddle boxes for years afterwards. The *Lucy Ashton* ended her days as the last example of the old arrangement in Clyde service, having outlasted all others by twenty years.

A flurry of construction during the nineties brought seven new steamers to Craigendoran within a decade, leaving the *Lucy Ashton* virtually the veteran of the North British fleet after the older ships of the seventies and eighties had been sold. It was a curious position for a fairly new boat, and reflected the advances in design which had been stimulated by unbridled competition during the railway era of Clyde steamer history. The *Lucy*, with small saloons, low-pressure boiler and single engine was fundamentally of an older period and the management felt that

65

her usefulness was limited. Tentative moves towards her disposal were made in 1900 but negotiations lapsed, probably because of unsatisfactory offers, so that the company changed its mind and decided to retain the little steamer. The *Lucy Ashton* was given a new boiler in 1901 and continued to sail on all-the-year-round services, having by this time deserted the Holy Loch for the Gareloch where she was to become a familiar sight for forty years.

Nevertheless, her career might well have been short had it not been for a fortuitous combination of circumstances. The first of these was the sale of one of her consorts, resulting in a shortage of steamers; the second was the occasion, also in 1901, when her engine suffered an unusually severe breakdown and was badly damaged. She was taken in hand by A. & J. Inglis, of Pointhouse, who fitted her with a new compound diagonal engine of conventional twin crank pattern – a very neat design similar to the firm's engines for contemporary Loch Lomond steamers. A high-pressure haystack boiler was provided, and the new boiler of 1901 thereupon transferred to another steamer. Thus transformed, the *Lucy Ashton* returned to service as one of the only two compound-engined steamers in the North British fleet, for this conservative company, with a view to lower capital costs, had favoured the almost obsolete single diagonal engine for new construction right up to 1898.

The *Lucy Ashton* was further altered in 1903 by the enlargement of her deck saloons and it seems strange that her fore-saloon was not carried out to the full width of the hull at that time. The practice was standard in other Clyde fleets and had been introduced in the North British company's own *Waverley* in 1899. Possibly it was felt that the ship's stability would have suffered, but whatever the reason the *Lucy Ashton* retained alleyways round the saloon and perpetuated this archaic feature until withdrawal.

A. & J. Inglis replaced the paddle boxes with new ones of their own handsome design when the ship's saloons were improved. They were smaller than the originals but, like them, had eight radial vents. The centrepiece was a bust of Lucy Ashton, surrounded by gilt thistles, and the name appeared in gilded lettering on the outer edge of the paddle box. Gone, however, was its ornamental gilded pillar, formerly a well known feature

David MacBrayne's beautiful *Grenadier* in Oban Bay. She appears to be lying off the railway pier for photographic purposes, and the fact that her pennants are at half-mast suggests the recent death of a company servant or public personality. The vessel is shown as rebuilt with haystack boilers in 1901–2. *G. E. Langmuir Collection*

The lovely *Lucy Ashton* arriving at Garelochhead, on the route which she made her own for so many years. This photograph shows the North British veteran as sailing in the 1920s and early 1930s. *John Crosby Collection*

The veteran *Lucy Ashton* in 1948, her last Clyde season, wearing the alien colours of British Railways. This photograph, taken at Craigendoran, shows the wheelhouse fitted during the 1939–45 war. *G. E. Langmuir*

of Craigendoran steamers. It was almost certainly at this time that the old stairways and sponson houses were abolished, the former being replaced by stairs to both saloons from the middle of the promenade deck, and the latter by modern lavatories.

In 1908 came the final stage in the vessel's modernisation when a companionway shelter was placed above the stair to the fore-saloon, and a combined shelter, purser's office and captain's cabin replaced the old cabin below the bridge. The *Lucy Ashton* had now reached virtually her final outline, the original hull having in effect been gutted and the steamer practically renewed as an efficient, modern general-purpose vessel.

Wartime and After

By 1914, the *Lucy*'s internal appointments were not really up to the standard of the ships built for the company in the later 1890s, although her new compound engine made it difficult to think of withdrawing her. However, it was decided in that year to order a replacement. Tenders were submitted by Wm Denny & Bros, Dumbarton, the Ailsa Shipbuilding Co Ltd, Troon, and A. & J. Inglis Ltd – the last-named builders receiving the order for a large, cruising paddle steamer designed as an improvement upon the *Waverley* of 1899. The intention of the North British directors was undoubtedly to replace the *Lucy Ashton* with one of the smaller ships in the fleet, and by a readjustment of duties to make room for the new vessel on the principal sailings out of Craigendoran. In the absence of written details one can only speculate on the disposal of the *Lucy Ashton*'s modern machinery, but it would have been surprising if it had not been installed in one of the company's larger steamers driven by single diagonal machinery – the *Dandie Dinmont, Talisman* or *Kenilworth*.

The North British arrangements of 1914 were far-seeing and imaginative, and the story of the *Lucy Ashton* would certainly have concluded shortly thereafter had it not been for the outbreak of World War I, when it was realised in Admiralty circles that shallow-draught paddle steamers were well adapted for minesweeping work and in due course most of the Clyde ships were requisitioned for that purpose. For instance the new North British vessel, *The Fair Maid*, was ideally suited for naval service in view of the fact that she had been built in wartime, and she was completed as an auxiliary warship, running her trials in the Gareloch in 1916. Her all too brief career ended disastrously later in the same year when she was sunk by a mine near Cross Sands Buoy, off Dover. The *Lucy Ashton* by this time had become firmly identified with the Craigendoran–Greenock ferry service as well as the Gareloch route. She was not requisitioned for war service and on her therefore fell the task of maintaining the North British sailings along with her junior consort, the *Dandie Dinmont*. Both steamers sailed only in the upper firth, for the construction of an anti-submarine boom between Dunoon and the Cloch in 1915 effectively prevented through sailings from Craigendoran to Rothesay. That traffic had to be abandoned to the Caledonian Steam Packet Company for the duration of the war, and it was not until 1919 that services reverted to a normal pattern on the removal of the boom and the return of the ships that had survived hostilities.

The post-war period revived the issue of the *Lucy Ashton*'s future. The marine superintendent, Captain Gilchrist, wrote to the North British general manager in June 1921 pointing out that her boiler required heavy repairs and that the Board of Trade surveyor would not pass it unless these were carried out. Authority was given to approach A. & J. Inglis Ltd for a quotation for a new haystack boiler, and the shipbuilders offered to provide one for £4,740 with a reduction of £420 if parts of the old boiler were good enough to be used again; but the railway company decided to delay the whole matter. The *Lucy Ashton* was accordingly nursed along for another year with minimal attention, but her condition in the summer of 1922 was giving 'considerable anxiety', according to Captain Gilchrist. The surveyor had required the working pressure to be reduced by 20psi and refused to allow her to sail for another season in her unsatisfactory state.

Faced with this ultimatum the company had to decide either to dispose of the vessel or order a new boiler. The marine superintendent felt the latter course to be desirable, but the general manager wanted several quotations. In the uneasy economic circumstances of the early twenties shipyard wages had been reduced and A. & J. Inglis Ltd now offered to supply a new boiler for £3,630, being £270 less than the quotation of their immediate neighbours, D. & W. Henderson of Meadowside. The matter was further delayed until the autumn of 1922, when Captain Gilchrist reported to the general manager that 'as the *Lucy Ashton* has the lowest registered tonnage of any steamer in the fleet and as it has also the lowest coal consumption, I would respectfully suggest that the question of retaining the vessel receive further consideration'. He was invited to report directly to the Locomotive Committee of the Board in mid-September and evidently convinced the directors, who authorised the order of a new boiler from A. & J. Inglis Ltd as well as various repairs to the hull costing a further £1,325, the additional work including replacement of the original wooden bulwarks on the fore deck by steel sheeting.

In this form the old steamer maintained the Gareloch service, year in, year out, summer and winter, and became something of an institution. Modern visitors to that area can hardly imagine what an attractive part of the Clyde the Gareloch was in the early twenties – quiet, peaceful, and wholly unspoiled by the ravages of military installations and industrial establishments. Nowadays, with its eastern shore abandoned to technical progress and suburbia sprawling to its very head, the backwater of yesteryear has changed, probably for ever. The author's mother remembered the old Gareloch where, with her sisters, she would disembark from the *Lucy Ashton* at the quiet little hamlet of Mambeg to spend holidays with a favourite aunt, recalling how the old paddle steamer was an integral part of the scene, so that everyone knew the captain and crew as friends, and how the *Lucy* sailed in, proudly dressed overall, on the day of a family wedding.

In the summer of 1936 the old North British colours, familiar on the Clyde for over half a century, were abruptly abandoned in favour of a startling new livery somewhat akin to that of the steamers of the erstwhile Glasgow & South Western Railway. The hull was painted grey, as were the paddle boxes, while saloons and deckhouses were white. The red, white and black funnel colours were retained, but lining and decoration were all but given up. The reason for the change was probably the pressing need for economies during the depression years of the thirties. The London & North Eastern Railway, into which the North British had been amalgamated in 1923, was particularly hard hit by the industrial slump and the change of steamer colours was simply an outward sign of retrenchment. The new livery was not liked, as the paint did not wear well and looked cheap. The *Lucy Ashton*, very much a Victorian steamer, looked particularly inappropriate in her new dress.

World War II

By the late thirties the ship was venerable, even by Clyde standards, and when she celebrated her golden jubilee in 1938 it was clear that her days were numbered. The Craigendoran fleet suffered severely the following season, only three vessels being commissioned for the summer services where two years earlier there had been six. The *Kenilworth*, last of the classic North British single diagonal paddle steamers, was broken up, and the *Waverley* (1899) and *Lucy Ashton* laid aside in Bowling harbour pending disposal. Rumours were rife that the LNER contemplated abandoning their Clyde steamer interests entirely, but the outbreak of World War II in September 1939 transformed the whole situation. With the exception of the *Lucy Ashton*, which was retained for the Craigendoran connections, the entire LNER fleet was immediately requisitioned for Admiralty duties. The Dunoon submarine boom was again a barrier dividing the estuary into upper and lower areas, so that the *Lucy Ashton*'s runs were fairly short, and her work-load was further relieved when the Gareloch was closed to ordinary sailings – permanently, as it transpired. But the little paddle steamer maintained a steady round to Gourock, Kilcreggan, Kirn and Dunoon throughout the whole of the wartime years, earning a splendid reputation for reliability and winning for herself a unique place in the annals of Clyde steamer history.

During all those terrible years she was out of service for only ten days, following damage to a paddle wheel in March 1944. Routine maintenance had to be carried out during weekends at the Inglis yard at Pointhouse. Unlike World War I, when peacetime liveries were retained, the *Lucy Ashton* was painted naval grey and signs of identification were removed in favour of the number D 56 painted on the bow. A concrete wheelhouse was added for the protection of the crew in the event of aerial attack, which understandably did nothing to enhance her lines, and in this nondescript guise she made her way round the firth. Her companion for most of the time was the Caledonian steamer *Marchioness of Lorne*, similarly clad in grey battledress, which maintained the connections from Gourock to Loch Long and the Holy Loch.

The end of the war in Europe allowed Craigendoran–Rothesay sailings to be resumed from July 1945, and the *Lucy Ashton* carried on the service until the return of the renovated *Jeanie Deans* in June of the following year. There was general satisfaction when the old colours of the North British Railway reappeared to replace the unpopular livery of the late thirties. In the case of the larger steamers there was considerable simplification as regards saloon and sponson panelling, but the *Lucy Ashton* was gradually, and without being withdrawn from service, repainted in a close approximation to her earlier style. The author therefore retains the most delightful memories of the veteran's gay and attractive appearance in 1946–7; during the war we had been starved of colour and the sight of the Craigendoran fleet in its old-time splendour was quite overwhelming to younger enthusiasts. The *Lucy Ashton* had lost her concrete bridge protection towards the end of the war, the final change in her outline being its replacement by a new wooden wheelhouse – the solitary Clyde example of a proper wheelhouse abaft of the funnel – and in that condition she sailed on into her Indian summer.

The summer of 1947 was incredibly fine, with long, hot days that brought traffic back to the Clyde in something like the old manner. Craigendoran saw the return of the diesel-electric *Talisman* as well as the *Jeanie Deans*, and then came the last paddle steamer for service on the firth, the new *Waverley* from the Inglis yard, inheritor of a great name and tradition. For the first time in a decade four paddle vessels occupied the berths at the LNER headquarters, a welcome and colourful sight after years of grey austerity. In midsummer the fleet visited the Clyde to be reviewed by the king. Every steamer was pressed into service for excursion cruises around the fleet and from the deck of the *Jeanie Deans* one recalls seeing the *Lucy Ashton*, resplendent in peacetime colours, sailing down the line of warships with an immense crowd of passengers in the calm of a perfect evening.

Diamond Jubilee

The year that followed, 1948, was the *Lucy Ashton*'s last in service, and marked her sixtieth anniversary, an astonishing record for such an unremarkable steamer. Two world wars had certainly contributed to prolonging her career far beyond the usual span, but for a ship which had spent much of her time sailing in summer and winter six decades was a tremendous achievement and in itself eloquent testimony to her usefulness. In recalling that the celebrated *Iona* outlasted the *Lucy Ashton* by twelve years one must remember that the MacBrayne steamer sailed throughout her life during the summer months only, and had much more money and care lavished upon her to ensure that her condition was as nearly perfect as possible. The *Lucy Ashton*, on the other hand, took the usual knocks and bangs of general service and received nothing like the same attention.

When Britain's railways were nationalised in 1948 it was plain that many long-established traditions would come to an end. The change for the Craigendoran steamers came early, when the attractive North British colours were finally abandoned in favour of the Caledonian Steam Packet Company's livery, which was adopted for the unified Clyde fleet. The *Lucy Ashton* was undergoing repair at Pointhouse early in the year and she was the first to appear in the unprepossessing buff and black funnel and plain white saloons of the new régime. It was a matter for general regret that the old ship should end her service in an alien garb, and many people felt that she might have been allowed to remain in Craigendoran colours to the end.

The undoubted highlight of the *Lucy Ashton*'s last season was her diamond jubilee cruise under the auspices of the Clyde River Steamer Club, on 29 May 1948. On a day of beautiful weather a trainload of passengers travelled from Glasgow Queen Street station behind the green D-11 class locomotive No 2680 *Lucy Ashton* down the line of the original Helensburgh railway to Craigendoran, there to board the veteran paddle steamer, gaily dressed overall for her triumphal progress across the firth. Few if any of those who saw her lying beside the new *Waverley* realised that the two graceful ships linked the high noon of Clyde paddle steamers and their final twilight; that in less than twenty-five years this type of excursion vessel and the trade on which it flourished would be on the verge of extinction. Fortunately, no such dismal thoughts spoiled the pleasure of the passengers, who enjoyed a cruise ranging round the upper firth, including a last trip up the *Lucy Ashton*'s own Gareloch, a call at the Caledonian rival's headquarters at Gourock, a final, nostalgic run round the lovely Holy Loch where the young *Lucy* had started her career in Queen Victoria's time, and a run down to Rothesay. There, in the Mecca of Clyde steamers, she lay for over an hour in glorious sunshine before breaking new ground at the end of her life by a cruise into Loch Striven, and finally turned again at last to her home port.

The *Lucy Ashton*'s remaining time was short. She sailed continuously throughout 1948 and into the following year until, at last, she made her final run from Dunoon to Craigendoran in February 1949. She was then despatched to Bowling Bay and moored in that well known haven of older Clyde steamers to await a decision as to her future. There were rumours, understood to have had some substance, that the ship would be given a new navy boiler; but the eventual order for her final withdrawal was inevitable. Proverbially, new wine seldom goes well into old bottles, and in the chilly financial climate of the early fifties expenditure in renovating an outworn steamer would have been rightly regarded as money wasted. The *Lucy Ashton* had given good service far beyond the normal average lifetime of a Clyde steamer and her owners were content to call it a day. She finished her career as it had begun, without undue ceremony, reliable to the very end. With no special features to commend her, quite unremarkable in performance, the *Lucy Ashton* nevertheless endeared herself to generations of passengers and ended her life as one of the great Clyde steamers of all time. Her story may hide a moral.

6

DUCHESS OF HAMILTON

Every now and again in the long history of Clyde passenger
steamers there appeared a vessel which was generally
acknowledged as an outstanding example of the best
contemporary design. The *Iona* and *Columba* typified the mid-
Victorian tourist steamer at its best, and the latter was never
really surpassed in many respects. The *Ivanhoe* of 1880 was the
harbinger of a general and long overdue improvement in Clyde
steamboat facilities, and that she could be made to operate
profitably without reliance on the sale of alcoholic refreshment
amazed the sceptics and assured her of a unique place in the
gallery of immortals. The successive steamers bearing the
romantic name *Lord of the Isles* were also superior to most other
ships of their time and remained great favourites with the public.
These vessels come readily to mind, but another which had equal
reputation in her own day tends now to be forgotten – the first
Duchess of Hamilton, that splendid paddle steamer built in 1890
for the Caledonian Steam Packet Company Ltd, and for many
years the acknowledged flagship of its fleet. Perhaps her
untimely end during World War I which prevented her becoming
known to a younger generation caused her reputation to fade,
perhaps it was simply due to there being so many 'crack'
steamers in the Caledonian fleet latterly; but whatever the
reason, she has seldom been accorded the respect still
commanded by some of her consorts.

Origins

The circumstances leading to the building of the *Duchess of
Hamilton* were complex. During the late 1880s the Lanarkshire
& Ayrshire Railway – a line sponsored by the Caledonian – was
constructed from Lugton, on the Glasgow, Barrhead &
Kilmarnock Joint Railway, to Ardrossan, where the existing

76

Robert Morton, designer of many of the finest Clyde paddle steamers, including the *Duchess of Hamilton* and *Neptune*. For several years he was in partnership with James Williamson, the firm of Morton & Williamson establishing a reputation as marine consultants not only on the Clyde but also in Australia. *The late Rev. Ralph Morton*

The Caledonian Steam Packet Company's flagship *Duchess of Hamilton* in her heyday on the Ardrossan–Arran service. *G. E. Langmuir Collection*

A deck view on board the *Duchess of Hamilton* during the Edwardian years. The steamer is swinging into Loch Long on a cruise from Gourock. A Volunteer band is prominent in the foreground of this splendid picture, which gives a delightful impression of the Edwardians at play. Note the parasols and the formality of the passengers' clothing — everyone is wearing a hat! *Author's Collection, by courtesy of Mr A. Fraser*

Captain James Williamson, Secretary and Manager of the Caledonian Steam Packet Company, Limited. He was one of the dominating figures in the long history of Clyde steamers and his flair for management and insistence upon high standards of design and service gave the Clyde fleet its pre-eminent place during the twenty-five years before the outbreak of World War I. *The Bailie–Mitchell Library, Glasgow*

harbour and associated works were at the same time being rebuilt and enlarged. The object was to enable the Caledonian Company to attract largely to itself the burgeoning foreign trade in Lanarkshire coal without passing it over the competing routes of the rival Glasgow & South Western Railway, save only for the latter concern's joint interest in the Barrhead line which was traversed in part by coal trains. The export trade of those years was very profitable and of itself amply justified the Caledonian Railway's outlay, but passenger traffic over the new route was not expected to be remunerative in an area where the Glasgow & South Western had long enjoyed a monopoly. Clearly, the Lanarkshire & Ayrshire promoters had the Irish passenger traffic more in mind, and to this end arrangements were made with Messrs G. & J. Burns to provide a 'daylight' steamer service between Ardrossan and Belfast. Montgomerie Pier at Ardrossan was extensively improved as a railhead for the new through traffic, which began in 1892.

Before 1890 the whole traffic between Glasgow and the Isle of Arran was worked by the South Western Company, whose trains connected at Ardrossan with Captain William Buchanan's steamer *Scotia*. It seems unlikely from the available evidence that the Caledonian plans originally envisaged competition in this area, but events further north apparently caused a change of intention. The company's Gourock extension was opened to traffic in June 1889 and the new facilities included a fleet of railway-controlled steamers. Here also there had been no idea of competing with private steamboat owners, but an approach by the railway directors offering rail connections at Gourock had been so unenthusiastically received that the Caledonian board set about establishing a fleet of their own with considerable vigour. We have previously noted their purchase of the *Meg Merrilies* and *Madge Wildfire* from the Campbells of Kilmun; in addition to those steamers, two new vessels were ordered from local shipyards, and a bill was introduced in Parliament seeking the necessary powers for the Caledonian Railway to operate services on the Firth of Clyde. When the House of Commons committee threw it out, the dismayed directors had no alternative but to form an independent concern to own and operate the ships, and in May 1889 the Caledonian Steam Packet Company Limited was registered to carry out these purposes in association with the railway company.

Once this step had been taken it seems likely that the impending completion of the new railway to Ardrossan suggested that the Arran trade might be won for the Caledonian, and as early as 27 August 1889 the Steam Packet Company's minutes recorded submission of a plan and specification of 'the proposed steamer for the Ardrossan & Arran traffic', indicating that consideration of the project had taken place earlier in the year. Plans were sufficiently advanced early in October for discussions to be held with the railway directors, resulting in a decision that specifications be issued and tenders invited for the building of a steamer for the Ardrossan and Arran traffic.

The Denny Contract

Five Clyde yards tendered for the new vessel and the contract was eventually given to the Dumbarton firm of Wm Denny & Bros, whose offer to build the steamer, as specified, for £24,400, was the lowest by a wide margin. The Dennys enjoyed a wide reputation in the shipbuilding world; by skill and high ability they came to occupy a unique position as specialist builders of cross-channel ships towards the close of the nineteenth century, and perhaps their most notable triumph was the construction of the world's first turbine-driven commercial vessel, the *King Edward*, in 1901. In earlier years they had been responsible for the completion of another outstanding ship, the tea clipper *Cutty Sark*, after the financial failure of Scott & Linton, a neighbouring builder; but these were but two highlights in an impressive succession of ships built for service in all parts of the world. Curiously, however, the firm's contribution to the Clyde passenger steamer fleet up to 1890 had been meagre, such few vessels as it had completed being turned out in the very early years of steam navigation on the firth.

No mention of the origins of the *Duchess of Hamilton* would be complete without reference to Robert Morton, a naval architect and consulting engineer of great ability and flair in the design of coastal steamers, who prepared the original plan and specifications and superintended her building. Formerly in partnership with Captain James Williamson in private practice – the latter resigning to join the Caledonian Steam Packet

Company late in 1888 – he had designed the first really modern paddle steamer in 1886 for Australian owners. The *Ozone*, built for Huddart, Parker & Co Ltd of Melbourne, was fitted with compound engines and navy boilers working under forced draught; her success was remarkable and created something of a sensation not only in Australia but also in marine engineering circles at home. The same principles were now incorporated into the design of the *Duchess of Hamilton*, with equal effect.

Dennys for their part had ideas for improving upon the original design which interested the Caledonian directors sufficiently to authorise James Williamson to discuss matters further, and on 23 October 1889 the builders submitted an alternative tender for a paddle steamer 250ft × 30ft × 10ft moulded, to be driven by compound diagonal machinery and fitted with 3 navy boilers, with a guaranteed speed of 17 knots. The price remained as in the original tender, but penalties were provided if speed should fall short of the guarantee, and rejection allowed in the event of its falling below 16 knots. Conversely, a premium at the rate of £3,000 for a full knot above the guarantee was provided for 'but under no circumstances is the cost of the vessel to exceed £27,400'. The revised offer was accepted and work began at once in the Leven shipyard.

For the time being, however, the owners were at considerable pains to conceal the fact that the new steamer was intended for their Clyde service, doubtless to prevent the Glasgow & South Western Railway learning of the threat to its Arran trade until too late to take effective counter-steps. Negotiations with the builders were conducted through the firm of Morton & Williamson as agents, and the steamer was referred to in correspondence as 'New Ozone' or 'Australia No 2' until February 1890. The newspapers reported that she was intended for the Antipodes, a rumour to which Morton & Williamson's Australian business connection gave effective support; and not until the spring of 1890 was it stated that she was in fact being built for the Caledonian Steam Packet Company.

Luxury Afloat

The hull of the *Duchess of Hamilton* was carefully designed to allow maximum beam in proportion to length within the limits necessitated by the guaranteed contract speed. The Denny testing tank, a pioneer British experimental venture in the field of hull design, was employed for this purpose, to excellent effect. The new steamer had unusually generous deck space and it was noteworthy that while the normal ratio of length to beam in older Clyde ships was about 10 to 1, in the case of the Denny vessel it fell to just over 8 to 1, thus allowing valuable increases in deck and saloon space as compared with an older steamer of the same length. A novel feature, made standard in all subsequent Caledonian steamers, was the continuation of the promenade deck forward to the bow, the main deck space below being left open instead of having the topside plating carried up to the top deck in the style that latterly became general in British pleasure steamers.

There was a very large saloon on the main deck aft and a smaller one forward, with alleyways round it to allow the deckhands to go about their work without disturbing passengers. Two small deckhouses, one carrying the bridge, were the only shelters on the promenade deck, and in bad weather accommodation on top was rather Spartan by modern standards. Below decks, however, all was luxury. The huge first-class saloon, equipped with sprung settees and reading and writing tables, was finished in walnut, with mahogany pilasters enriched by hand-painted gilt panels, the ceiling being panelled in wood and finished in cream and gold. The floor was laid with carpets and runners, and spring blinds and curtains in terra cotta and tan completed the decoration of a saloon which had few rivals in Clyde service. The first-class dining saloon on the lower deck aft seated ninety people, mainly in groups of four round individual tables, an arrangement vastly superior to the institutional rows of communal boards customary in the declining years of the British coastal excursion steamer. The decoration was pale blue, with upholstery in old-gold frieze velvet, the specification requiring 'all to be thoroughly painted and tastefully relieved with rich gilded work'.

Steerage accommodation was forward, in accordance with the universal practice of the time, the main deck saloon having room for a hundred passengers in much plainer surroundings than the first-class travellers. There was also a smoking room, handsomely upholstered in buffalo hide, and other facilities included a special cabin for ladies. Lavatory accommodation for both sexes was immeasurably superior to the inadequate facilities encountered in the older type of Clyde steamer; there was even a bath available, but this feature was a rarity and not really necessary in view of the relatively short distances covered by the steamer. However, no doubt the provision was appreciated by travellers crossing to Arran after all-night journeys from the south.

Modern Machinery

The machinery of the *Duchess of Hamilton* was unique on the Clyde, albeit absolutely characteristic of the practice of Denny & Co, her builders' engineering associates. The engine was a compound diagonal incorporating valve gear adapted by Walter Brock, managing director of Wm Denny & Bros, from the Walschaerts motion so familiar on modern steam locomotives, and it involved the use of a distinctive pattern of framing, tilted sharply towards the cylinders to provide convenient bearings for the expansion links. This arrangement was said to facilitate overhaul by making the valves more readily accessible, but the only other example of its use on the Clyde was in the *Caledonia* (1934). Four cast-steel entablatures were specified for the *Duchess of Hamilton*, together with a built-up crankshaft of Siemens-Martin ingot steel – later Caledonian steamers had solid-forged crankshafts. The paddle wheels had seven feathering floats of best elm, the diameter over floats being 17ft.

Steam was supplied by three navy boilers working at a pressure of 110psi in a closed stokehold under forced draught. The largest was 10ft 2in in diameter, with three furnaces, and the others were 8ft 4in in diameter with two furnaces each, all being coal-fired and having uptakes into a single funnel. The problem of soot and ashes falling over the deck was alleviated to some extent by incorporation of the Denny and Brace spark arrester in the uptakes, a device much used by the Dumbarton yard at that period. Externally its presence was revealed by the distinctive funnel base, a feature shared with the Belle steamers on the Thames which were also equipped with the apparatus.

Reference to the London fleet recalls the strong family resemblance of the Caledonian flagship to those vessels, all of which were built in Dumbarton. They shared a design of paddle box almost unique amongst Scottish steamers, the only other one to embody this standard Denny pattern being the *Marchioness of Lorne*, built by Russell & Co of Port Glasgow in the following year very much along the lines of her larger sister. The boxes carried no nameboards, contrary to common Clyde practice, but the rather wide border was relieved by a number of small ports. The main panel consisted of horizontal slots that formed a backcloth to the centrepiece, the magnificently carved, painted and gilded coat of arms of the Hamilton family, proprietors of the Island of Arran.

The paddle box of the *Duchess of Hamilton*

The *Duchess of Hamilton* was launched on 10 April 1890 by Miss L. Thompson, daughter of Mr (later Sir) James Thompson, general manager of the Caledonian Railway. Six weeks later the ship was completed and on 28 May ran speed trials between the Cloch and Cumbrae lighthouses, attaining 18.1 knots as the mean of two runs over the distance, thus handsomely exceeding the guaranteed speed stipulated in the building contract and earning the full premium of £3,000 for Wm Denny & Bros. On the following day she conveyed a party of specially invited guests outwards by the Kyles of Bute to Whiting Bay and back by the Garroch Head to Gourock. Lunch was served, and many congratulatory speeches made by the well-satisfied builders and owners. Approaching Kirn, the steamer was slowed to wait for MacBrayne's *Columba* returning from Ardrishaig and the new *Duchess* succeeded in winning the subsequent brisk race to Gourock, in this way setting the seal on the success of the Caledonian flagship.

The Arran Run

The Caledonian Railway's service to Arran began on 30 May 1890 and the company clearly attached much importance to its new route. An entirely new train, the Arran Express, had been built at St Rollox to the designs of Dugald Drummond, the locomotive, carriage and wagon superintendent. Made up of eight bogie carriages, the new train captured immediate attention by its novel and beautiful livery of chocolate brown with white upper panels, the first example of the colours which thenceforth were standardised and became so familiar. Heading the train was the celebrated 4–4–0 express locomotive No 124 which had been built by Dubs & Co of Glasgow, virtually to Drummond's design, for display at the Edinburgh International Exhibition of Science, Industry and Art in 1886. She was one of the most modern engines in the company's service and that she should have been transferred to the Ardrossan route and given the rare distinction of a name, *Eglinton*, was sufficient indication of the directors' interests in ensuring the maximum publicity for the new service.

The first departure from Glasgow Central on the opening day was at 4.45pm and delay in transferring luggage at Montgomerie Pier caused the *Duchess of Hamilton* to be eighteen minutes late in arriving at Brodick. There followed an immediate instruction that heavy luggage for Arran should be sent by an earlier train to avoid delaying the steamer. The practice in 1890 was to stop trains at Eglinton Street (Glasgow) for ticket collection, and thereafter run non-stop to Ardrossan. As the service settled down into a routine the regular Glasgow to Brodick time of ninety minutes was kept without difficulty and in July 1891 a newspaper correspondent noted that out of nine normal weekday up morning runs during that month, only once had the scheduled time been exceeded and that only by two minutes.

One can imagine a summer day in 1890 as the Caledonian Railway's Arran Express approaches Ardrossan and its passengers prepare to change to the steamer for Brodick. The handsome blue express engine *Eglinton* swings through a cutting with its train of freshly painted carriages, runs past engine shed and sidings and, with safety valves lifting, sweeps through the

TO ISLAND OF ARRAN,
Via ARDROSSAN.

Commencing TO-DAY (SATURDAY), 31st Current, the Caledonian Company will Run an EXPRESS SERVICE OF TRAINS between GLASGOW (Central Station) and ARDROSSAN, in connection with the New Saloon Steamer DUCHESS OF HAMILTON, to and from ARRAN, the Journey being accomplished in 90 minutes.

The Train and Steamboat Service will be as under :—

GLASGOW TO ARDROSSAN.

		A.	B.	
	A.M.	P.M.	P.M.	P.M.
Glasgow (Central Station), Dep..	8.45	1.45	4.45	5.13
,, (Eglinton St. Station), ,,	8.49	1.49	4.49	5.16
Ardrossan Station........Arrive	9.34	2.28	—	6.10
,, Pier .... ,,	9.35	2.30	5.30	6.12
,, Pier ....Depart	9.40	2.35	5.35	6.20
Brodick ....Arrive	10.20	3.15	6.15	7.0
Lamlash .... ,,	10.40	3.35	6.35	7.20
Whiting Bay .... ,,	11.0	3.55	6.55	7.40

ARDROSSAN TO GLASGOW.

	C.	D.			A.
	A.M.	A.M.	P.M.	P.M.	P.M.
Whiting Bay ..Depart	6.50	7.5	12.30	3.15	4.15
Lamlash ...... ,,	7.10	7.25	12.50	3.35	4.35
Brodick ...... ,,	7.30	7.45	1.10	3.55	4.55
Ardrossan Pier..Arrive	8.10	8.25	1.50	4.25	5.35
Ardrossan Pier..Depart	8.15	8.30	1.55	4.40	5.40
,, Station ,,	—	—	2.0	4.43	5.45
Glas.(Eglin.St.Sta.)D'p	8.56	9.12	2.59	5.36	6.31
,, (Central Sta'n.)Arr.	9.0	9.15	3.3	5.40	6.35

A. Saturdays only.	C. Mondays only.
B. Daily except Saturdays.	D. Daily except Mondays.

DAILY EXCURSIONS are made (Saturday excepted) from ARDROSSAN and the ARRAN PORTS to AILSA CRAIG, ROUND ARRAN, ROUND BUTE, or to CAMPBELTOWN, from Ardrossan on arrival of the 8.45 A.M. Train from Glasgow (Central Station).

RETURN FARES—

	1st Class and Steamer.	3d Class and Steamer.
Glasgow and Arran........	5s 6d	3s 9d
Do. Excursion....	7s	5s
Ardrossan and Arran........Cabin, 2s.		Steerage, 1s 6d.
Do. Excursion.... ,, 3s.		,, 2s.
Arran and Do. ,, 2s.		,, 1s 6d.

The Trip on MONDAY, 2d June, will be ROUND AILSA CRAIG, and on TUESDAY ROUND ARRAN, WEDNESDAY to CAMPBELTOWN.

CIRCULAR TOUR Daily going via GOUROCK or WEMYSS BAY and returning via ARDROSSAN or vice versa.

Caledonian Steam Packet Co., Limited,
302 Buchanan Street, Glasgow.

The inaugural Caledonian service to Arran in 1890

town station and down to the harbour where it draws to a halt at Montgomerie Pier. Passengers have no time to linger on this, the principal competing service for the Arran traffic against the Glasgow & South Western Railway, whose train is even now arriving at Winton Pier, just across the harbour. They are hustled from the carriages to the pier and on board the steamer which is to carry them to Brodick. In three minutes they hear the quick clang of engine-room telegraphs, the gangways are pulled ashore, ropes cast clear, and the *Duchess of Hamilton* is away for Arran. The beat of her paddle floats speeds up as she heads out past the breakwater and towards the distant blue island mountains, while astern the two black funnels of the *Scotia* lay down a smoke screen as she ineffectually pursues the new Caledonian steamer.

Racing Days

The *Duchess of Hamilton* was commanded from the outset by Robert Morrison, formerly of the Anchor Line. He had been mate in that company's vessel *Utopia* and must have regarded his translation as a fortunate move when, not long afterwards, his old ship was sunk in a collision in the harbour at Gibraltar with appalling loss of life. On the Clyde, events were less tragic, but elements of drama occasionally enlivened 'the daily round, the common task'. Competition with Buchanan's *Scotia* and the Glasgow & South Western Railway was fierce, despite the overwhelming advantages in favour of the Caledonian route. Captain Morrison's enthusiasm led to agonised correspondence in the newspapers, particularly after one famous morning when some sixty passengers were left at Whiting Bay ferry and twenty or so on Brodick pier because of over-precipitate departures by the *Duchess of Hamilton*.

Travellers were also put to much inconvenience on 22 July 1890 when the steamer broke down twice during her afternoon sailing from Brodick. The first incident involved only a damaged paddle float, but the second was more serious. Two miles off Ardrossan a steam-pipe burst and the vessel was unable to proceed, drifting instead rapidly down channel. The *Scotia* appeared at this stage but her captain's offer of assistance was declined, the Ardrossan harbour tug having by then come to the aid of the disabled *Duchess*. She was anchored and her passengers ferried ashore in relays. The connecting train, due to leave Ardrossan at 5.40, left in fact nearly five hours late and arrived in Glasgow around midnight.

The *Scotia* was encountered in more violent circumstances on 29 August of the same year when a collision took place between the two steamers at the narrow entrance to Ardrossan harbour. The Buchanan vessel had left Brodick ten minutes before the *Duchess of Hamilton* but the gap between the rivals gradually closed until, on the approach to Ardrossan, the latter was just drawing ahead. Off the breakwater the *Scotia* rammed the Caledonian steamer's paddle box, forcing her out of course and almost causing her in turn to ram a large barge lying at Montgomerie Pier. The incident led to a court case in 1891, when the owner of the *Scotia* was awarded damages, responsibility for the accident being attributed to the master of the *Duchess of Hamilton*.

Despite a gallant performance against great odds, the little *Scotia* was manifestly outclassed, and loss of traffic on this and other routes led the Glasgow & South Western Railway to provide its own steamers in 1892. Thus, after two seasons of having things very much her own way, the *Duchess of Hamilton* was faced by the new *Neptune*, a steamer of comparable standards and speed and, later in the same year, the great *Glen Sannox* – magnificent, costly, beautiful, and more than a match for the Caledonian vessel.

The *Duchess of Hamilton*, however, was really the better all-round ship for Clyde service, but even she was expensive to run on the Arran station. The Caledonian Steam Packet Company's minutes contained a detailed analysis of her service during 1891 when, of course, she was employed during the summer months only, spending 118 days in service and sailing 13,583 miles. A total of 88,731 passengers was carried at an average fare of 11s 9d each but while average earnings per mile were 6s 5¾d, expenses amounted to 8s 3¼d. The *Duchess of Hamilton* was an extravagant ship to run, costing about three times as much as the smaller units of the Caledonian fleet, and when it is appreciated that she carried fewer passengers annually than any of her consorts, it is scarcely surprising to learn that she operated at a loss even in the seasons before the *Glen Sannox* appeared on the same station. The trouble was that the Arran traffic never built up to the same extent as trade in the upper reaches of the Clyde. The island's population, largely Gaelic-speaking in the nineties, was engaged to a great extent in crofting and fishing, and successive Dukes of Hamilton, anxious to preserve amenity, had discouraged speculative building and tourism. Consequently, the island retained something of a Hebridean character until well into the twentieth century, and passenger traffic never developed on a scale sufficient to justify the lavish service provided by the railway companies before their rationalisation schemes came into effect after 1900.

A steamer as finely appointed as the *Duchess of Hamilton* was however constantly in demand for private charters and in course of time she became the regular, favourite 'club' steamer during the Clyde Fortnight, that great annual yachting event of bygone years. For this duty her crew dressed in white naval-style jerseys bearing the name of the ship woven across the chest. Each summer, for a few glorious days, 'society' trod her decks as the steamer followed the great racing yachts to the accompaniment of music from the orchestras and military bands which were invariably engaged on those occasions. Amidst the legendary contenders for the yachting trophies – the three *Valkyries*, *Britannia, Meteor, Satanita* and Sir Thomas Lipton's successive *Shamrocks* – the pride of the Caledonian fleet was as smartly turned out as any of them.

Latter Years

The *Duchess of Hamilton*'s activities changed considerably in 1906 when she was superseded on the Arran station by the turbine steamer *Duchess of Argyll*. Being due for reboilering, she was renovated by the Clyde Shipbuilding & Engineering Co at a cost of £2,350 and made her base thereafter at Gourock whence she sailed on general excursions and railway connections. Captain Morrison retired at this time and was succeeded by Captain Allan MacDougall. No striking incidents are recorded of her later career and the impression remains of a ship growing old gracefully. The years passed until the outbreak of World War I when, early in 1915, she was requisitioned by the Admiralty for service as an auxiliary minesweeper. Her peacetime colours

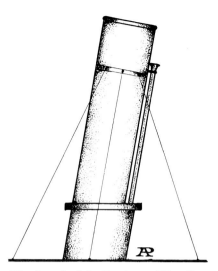

The funnel of the *Duchess of Hamilton*

disappeared under a coat of warship grey, but fortunately the splendid crests were removed from her paddle boxes before she went to war and remain in existence to this day.

Late in November 1915 the *Duchess of Hamilton* came to grief, being sunk by a mine. She had sailed for just over twenty-five years, a short span by the standards of steamers such as the *Iona* and *Lucy Ashton,* but it covered exactly the great years of the Clyde and its steamers. She would probably have been renovated for post-war service had she survived and could have been expected to continue sailing well into the 1920s. Fate decreed otherwise, however, and in one respect it was perhaps as well. This fine ship had been the pride of the Caledonian fleet for too long for those who knew her to contemplate lightly the prospect of her trudging round the firth in general service in the combined fleet of the London, Midland & Scottish Railway amidst the declining standards of a post-war world. Her best years were over when she went off to war where, like many of her human contemporaries, she perished, to the widespread regret of all who had known her in her prime. She had been the favourite of a lost generation and something of her high reputation died with her and those who had sailed in her. When she disappeared, something of the Clyde's old gaiety vanished for ever.

7

NEPTUNE

The handsome ships of the Glasgow & South Western Railway were amongst the most popular on the Firth of Clyde during the quarter of a century ending in 1914, a period in which the classic Clyde paddle steamer was improved to a high peak of efficiency. Gaily attired in a strikingly attractive livery, the 'Sou' West' boats competed fiercely and with a fair degree of success against their Caledonian and North British rivals. One of the first to enter service was the *Neptune*, a good-looking, speedy steamer intended for the company's Rothesay service. She has long been almost forgotten by all save those who knew her in her prime for, like the *Duchess of Hamilton* of the Caledonian fleet, she fell victim to a German mine in World War I and remained but a name to later generations of travellers.

New Shipowners

The Glasgow & South Western Railway came late to Clyde steamer operation. For years the company owned railheads at Greenock, Fairlie and Ardrossan, where its trains connected with privately owned steamboats sailing to most of the coastal resorts. It is probable that these arrangements might have continued indefinitely but for the overwhelming impact of Caledonian competition in 1889–90, which resulted in an alarming reduction of coast traffic by the South Western routes. As we have seen, drastic remedies were sought to counter the trend. In the short term, private owners were temporarily subsidised until arrangements could be made to obtain Parliamentary powers for the railway company to operate its own vessels. This achieved, several older steamers were acquired as the nucleus of a fleet, orders were placed for three new paddle steamers, and the railway services were accelerated and improved by the provision of new rolling stock. Lastly, the enlargement of Prince's Pier at Greenock was put in hand to provide a railhead comparable to the Caledonian's at Gourock.

The choice of marine superintendent fell on Captain Alexander Williamson, brother of the Caledonian Steam Packet Company's manager, and for twenty years the Clyde enjoyed the spectacle of a fraternal professional feud. The first task of the new superintendent was to review the fleet of old vessels under his command and advise on the building of new tonnage. This was done swiftly, and within a month of his appointment in August 1891 Captain Williamson was in a position to report to the directors and recommend the employment of Mr Robert Morton to design new steamers and prepare the necessary specifications.

At this time Morton was probably the leading marine designer and consultant in his field, with a reputation far beyond the Firth of Clyde. As principal of the firm of Morton & Williamson, and former partner of the Caledonian Steam Packet Company's manager, his friendship with the family, quite as much as professional competence, might have led Captain Alexander Williamson to suggest that he be invited to design the new Glasgow & South Western steamers. The plain fact was that there was no room for failure. The company had to be sure that its ships could steam faster than their Caledonian competitors in order to recover the traffic lost in 1889–91, and Robert Morton's reputation guaranteed that their requirements would be met. He certainly lost no time, presenting plans and specifications to the Steam Vessels Committee of the South Western board at the end of September and the directors 'agreed that Tenders should be asked according to the Specifications and plans submitted, and that Builders should also be asked to offer for any modification of these plans or on a design of their own which would give an increased guaranteed speed'.

Several tenders for new steamers were considered in mid-October and David Rowan & Son's offer to build a vessel for the Greenock and Rothesay service was accepted. This engineering firm sub-contracted the building of the ship herself to Napier, Shanks & Bell of Yoker, retaining the machinery and boiler contract for themselves in accordance with common practice on Clydeside. Rankin & Blackmore of Greenock, and Hutson & Corbett of Kelvinhaugh, were particularly noted for this system.

Robert Morton was appointed to superintend construction of the new ship 'the remuneration to him to be at the rate of not exceeding £5 5s per week'. By the end of October he had additional responsibilities, for the directors decided to have a duplicate steamer built and so it came about that the subject of this chapter, the *Neptune*, was one of a pair of twins, not a very common thing on the Clyde although there were several examples in the railway fleets at various times. Having this further work on his hands, as well as inspecting progress on the company's new Arran steamer, Morton's remuneration was revised by mutual agreement, a minute of the Steam Vessels Committee of 27 October 1891 recording that 'The Chairman ... reported having seen Mr. Robert Morton with reference to the inspection of the new Steamers, and the arrangement that he should inspect the Steamers on payment of $1\frac{1}{4}\%$ of the contract price, which would be held to include the preparing of plans and specifications, &c., already supplied to the Company, which was approved.'

Robert Morton modelled the new Glasgow & South Western steamer on the successful *Lorna Doone*, built to his specification by the same contractors earlier in 1891 for service on the Bristol Channel. She was of a design eminently suitable for the Clyde – a saloon steamer driven by twin crank compound machinery at a speed of around $17\frac{1}{2}$ knots. In adapting the prototype, Morton retained her main dimensions of 220.5ft length and 26ft breadth, but replaced the *Lorna Doone*'s narrow fore-saloon with a larger one carried out to the bulwarks to provide greater covered accommodation and, incidentally, rather improving the appearance. The high-pressure cylinder of the *Neptune* was made slightly larger, and other alterations were stipulated to increase the contract speed. Conditions were strict, the vessel being required to maintain $17\frac{3}{4}$ knots during a period of four hours' continuous steaming round the firth, while the measured mile off Skelmorlie was to be run twice during her trials to confirm that the speed was attained.

Construction and Trials

The *Neptune* was launched on 10 March 1892 by Miss Helen Barclay, daughter of a Glasgow & South Western Railway director, and ran trials only eighteen days later. As the first of the new steamers built for the company she attracted considerable attention, being favourably praised for her handsome appearance and excellent performance. She achieved a mean of 18 knots on two runs between the Cloch and Cumbrae lights, to the mutual satisfaction of builders and owners, and Robert Morton also must have been well satisfied with his improved *Lorna Doone*. Trials of the *Neptune*'s sister ship, the *Mercury*, later in the year produced a curious result. Built to identical specification by the same shipbuilders and engineers, she improved upon her twin's trial speed by $\frac{3}{4}$ knot and was always regarded as the livelier ship of the two.

The *Neptune* began service on 31 May 1892 by conveying a party of invited guests on a cruise in the firth, the beautiful spring weather matching the satisfaction of those on board as they enjoyed the customary dinner, accompanied by many toasts and eulogistic speeches. The remarks were well justified, for the *Neptune* was a splendid ship by the standards of her time, and lavishly fitted out to win back traffic lost to the Caledonian. The *Glasgow Herald* reported that her first-class saloon, on the main deck aft, was decorated 'in the best possible taste' with everything that could add to the comfort of passengers, including Brussels carpets, dainty damask curtains, and a handsome tiled Carron fireplace for use in winter. The first-class dining saloon, situated on the lower deck aft, was also richly decorated and furnished, and seated seventy passengers. The steerage saloon forward was more severely furnished with spar seats round the sides and a double settee in the centre. Immediately below was a second-class dining saloon, while the crew's quarters were in the forepeak. Unlike the *Lorna Doone*, the *Neptune* carried her navigating bridge on a combined purser's office and captain's cabin between the paddle boxes, abaft the funnel, following traditional Clyde practice.

The machinery was of particular interest and followed largely that of the *Lorna Doone*. The main feature was the provision of four entablatures of equal size, each pair enclosing a crank and set of eccentrics. It was a layout which found little favour, being rapidly displaced by the more popular type with two small entablatures outside and a large one in the centre. The intention in the *Neptune*, as in the *Lorna Doone*, was to secure maximum

The paddle box of the *Neptune*

strength with minimum weight and the engine framing was therefore made of cast steel, but in both ships the limits had been too narrowly approached. The Glasgow & South Western steamers had their entablatures stiffened during the first season, while the *Lorna Doone*'s machinery was in such a condition by 1898 that it had to be taken down and completely re-erected. The *Neptune* was equipped with two navy boilers working at a pressure of 115psi under forced draught in a closed stokehold. Each had three furnaces with uptakes carried into a single, well-proportioned funnel.

The *Neptune* was painted in the attractive new colours chosen for the South Western fleet, which had already drawn much favourable comment when applied to the second-hand ships acquired in 1891. Above a red underbody, the hull was painted dove grey with white saloons, sponson houses and paddle boxes, while the funnel was scarlet with black top. Deckhouses were the usual varnished teak, and lifeboats white. It was an outstandingly beautiful colour scheme, which lightened the appearance of an otherwise heavy looking hull. The paddle boxes were attractive, with the Glasgow & South Western crest on a circular panel as centrepiece, while the same device also appeared on the company's blue house flag.

The Nineties

Payment of the sum of £19,164 for building the *Neptune* was made to Messrs Rowan in April 1892. The first of the new Glasgow & South Western vessels to be put into commission, no time was lost in placing her on the important Ardrossan–Arran route on which, as we have seen, the Caledonian *Duchess of*

Hamilton had enjoyed great success since 1890. The little Buchanan steamer *Scotia* then maintaining the South Western connections was no match for her magnificent rival, and in the face of rapidly dwindling traffic her owner had been induced to retain his vessel on the station only by cash subsidies from the railway company. Such stopgap measures merely ensured continuance of the service until new ships were ready, and it was doubtless with relief that the South Western directors took delivery of the *Neptune* and arranged to accelerate the Glasgow–Brodick service from the beginning of May 1892. The new steamer was an excellent match for the Caledonian flagship and ding-dong racing was the order of the day from the moment of her arrival at Ardrossan.

That there was recklessness in the conduct of the service is apparent from newspaper correspondence of the period; an alarmed traveller communicated his fears to the *Glasgow Herald* during May with

> . . . It may be gratifying to the respective companies to know that on a Monday morning lately the steamer belonging to A left Brodick Pier three minutes later than the steamer belonging to B, and, notwithstanding this, A steamer arrived at exactly the same time at Ardrossan as B steamer; but it is to be considered, on the other hand, that both steamers were running side by side with each other nearly all the way to Ardrossan at a high pressure of steam, having each a large complement of passengers, whose lives, I think, were somewhat endangered should anything have taken place. I do hope the proper authorities will see to this at once, and if need be alter the hour of sailings.

Such letters were, of course, blandly ignored by 'the proper authorities'. Prestige was important to the South Western board, anxious to recover traffic lost to the Caledonian, and the risks inherent in racing were, if not ignored entirely, at least taken fairly lightly. Nevertheless, they did exist, as had been proved towards the end of April when the *Neptune*, entering Ardrossan harbour at full tilt, could not be reversed in time and collided with Montgomerie Pier, badly damaging her bow. After repairs she resumed her station and, still living dangerously, contrived to avoid further trouble until June when the *Glen Sannox* arrived to take over the Arran service and the *Neptune* retired to the upper firth.

By this time the sister ship *Mercury* was ready and both vessels began a regular service between Prince's Pier, Rothesay, and the Kyles of Bute. The pattern was altered in 1894 when Glasgow & South Western Railway arrangements were much expanded on completion of the enlarged and improved railhead at Prince's Pier. The *Neptune* was the steamer chosen to inaugurate a new service from Greenock to Arran by way of the Kyles of Bute, in direct competition with the privately owned excursion steamer *Ivanhoe*, of 1880. It was a strategic move which gave the initiative to the South Western company; the *Ivanhoe*, conducted on temperance principles with much success under the managership of Captain James Williamson, had made for herself a great reputation and a profitable trade which the *Neptune*, the more modern ship, now proceeded to erode. The *Ivanhoe*, for her part, was being run almost as an honorary member of the Caledonian Steam Packet Company's fleet, and the result of opposition from Prince's Pier was that through bookings from the Caledonian Railway system to Arran began to fall away. South Western traffic correspondingly increased, to such an extent as to justify building a larger and finer steamer, *Jupiter*, in 1896, forcing the Caledonian to assume direct ownership of the *Ivanhoe* in the following season and replace her in turn with a modern ship.

The *Neptune*, thus superseded, was transferred to a new station. The 'auld toon' of Ayr was a focal point of the Glasgow & South Western system and it seemed that a programme of summer excursions from the harbour offered excellent prospects of success. These were accordingly advertised to begin in July 1896 and ranged widely over the Firth of Clyde to Arrochar and Lochgoilhead, Ormidale, the Gareloch, Arran, Girvan and Stranraer. There were also evening cruises to Brodick, Pladda, Culzean Bay and Turnberry, as well as occasional daytime trips to follow the great yacht races which were so much a feature of the Clyde scene. Many of the excursions, in particular those to Arran and Stranraer, took the *Neptune* into exposed waters, and in time it was found necessary to substitute steel plating for the foremost observation windows of the forward saloon. No doubt there had been instances of smashed windows in heavy seas. Protective plating had also been added at an earlier stage round the forward sponson openings to prevent large waves breaking inboard, and with these details it became possible at last to distinguish the *Neptune* and *Mercury* from each other.

Edwardian Years

Both vessels were made subjects of an experiment in smoke control during 1902. One of the worst features of Clyde steamboat travel during the nineteenth century was 'the smoke fiend', railed against alike by travellers, local residents and newspapers. Good Scottish coal was available in abundance for steamers and it was burned in huge quantities in the inefficient marine boilers of the day. There was little incentive to improve matters as long as fuel remained cheap, and several experiments of earlier years were aimed at the substantial reduction or suppression of the vast volumes of smoke which often hung over the firth in palls rather than at fuel economy for its own sake. True, there were local bylaws which could be invoked against offenders, but no positive incentive encouraged owners to improve matters, and in the absence of compulsory legislation the majority were content to let things drift.

Introduction of navy boilers and forced draught proved something of a mixed blessing, for these were often worked at maximum capacity in the years when steamboat competition was at its height, and no captain would sacrifice half a knot of extra speed merely to prevent a cloud of smoke. Conditions at Prince's Pier were unusually bad in the early years, for the railway company's engine shed was close to the terminus and the unhappy residents of Greenock's west end enjoyed fumes from locomotives as well as from steamers. Provost Rodger raised the matter at a Police Board meeting as early as June 1892, stating that the nuisance from steamers was then nearly as bad as from locomotives. 'Residents', he said, 'had a painful time of it, and sick persons had positively little chance to improve.' Nevertheless, no attempts to improve the situation appear to have been made until the Glasgow & South Western Railway decided to try out an ingenious device patented by the British Fuel Economiser & Smoke Preventor Company Ltd, which they called a 'Bunsen Bridge'.

The principle of the invention was to draw pre-heated air by means of steam jets through a cast-iron bridge within the boiler furnace, thus increasing the temperature of the hot gases. Somewhat akin to the water-gas process, it was claimed to achieve high boiler efficiency by the complete combustion of fuel and virtual elimination of smoke. Fitted on board the *Mercury* in March, and the *Neptune* in July, 1902, the invention appeared to do all that was expected of it when the former ship ran trials in April, but as no subsequent reference has come to light in the company's surviving records it has to be presumed that the experiment was not pursued, either on the grounds of royalty costs, or of eventual failure materially to solve the smoke problem.

The *Neptune* was showing signs of wear and tear in 1912. A report by the marine superintendent in February stated that the boilers, funnel and promenade deck from forward of the chart house to the end of the fore-saloon would require renewal at the end of the season, and recommended the installation of electric light, a shelter screen over the stairs leading from the top deck to the main saloon and a similar shelter forward. Tenders were invited for the work, and the contract was eventually awarded to the Clyde Shipbuilding & Engineering Company Ltd of Port Glasgow, who offered to undertake it for the sum of £4,222 10s.

On her reappearance in the following season the *Neptune* was a much altered ship. A new, well-raked funnel, larger than the original one of 1892 and, abaft of it, a combined charthouse and shelter over the stairway, changed the vessel's profile. Surprisingly, the bridge was not moved forward of the funnel in accordance with what had become general Clyde practice by 1913, but remained in its old position between the paddle boxes. The remaining space on the roof of the new deck structure was given over to extra life-saving equipment demanded by the Board of Trade following the *Titanic* disaster of the previous year. A third lifeboat had also to be provided, and was placed on the starboard side at the after end of the promenade deck. External changes were completed by the provision of a small teak deck shelter over the companionway ahead of the funnel. In her altered condition the *Neptune* looked heavier, almost matronly, in comparison with the quite slim outline of twenty years earlier, but the changes undoubtedly made for a more imposing appearance. In view of common practice in more modern steamers of the time one wonders why the promenade deck was not carried forward and her bow plated up, but in most instances when vessels were so altered the speed was adversely affected and it was probably wiser to leave well alone.

Lost on Active Service

Under normal circumstances the *Neptune* would have sailed for many more years on the Clyde but her career was unexpectedly interrupted by the outbreak of World War I in August 1914. As with so many other ships of her type she was quickly commandeered by the Royal Navy for service as an auxiliary minesweeper, along with her sister the *Mercury*, and both served as such for most of the war, the *Neptune* being renamed *Nepaulin* and stationed at Dover. While on a sweep off Gravelines on 20 April 1917 she was blown up by a mine and sank with the loss of eighteen of her crew, sharing the unhappy fate of her old rival, the *Duchess of Hamilton*, a few months earlier. The *Mercury* survived the war years but had her bow and stern blown off in separate incidents and was fortunate to reach port again.

The work of the peacetime pleasure steamers during both world conflicts was of great importance, and their contribution to the war effort has scarcely been given the recognition it deserves. These ships were intended to work in fair weather conditions and that they and their crews rose so nobly to the challenge of naval service in all weathers, for much of the time in considerable danger, says much for their designers as well as the courage of those who sailed in them.

8

WAVERLEY

Clyde railway steamers as a group were generally popular ships. More money was spent on them than private owners could usually afford, and in consequence they were faster and better equipped than their up-river contemporaries, save for a few notable exceptions. There was normally little to pick and choose between one railway boat and another as far as the travelling public was concerned, but sometimes a steamer even in those well maintained fleets stood out as an outstanding example of a river craft and it is with one such vessel that this chapter is concerned.

The apparent conservatism of the North British Steam Packet Company, already noticed in the case of the *Lucy Ashton*, became more marked during the nineties, extending to the perpetuation of features which were fast becoming obsolete. Among these, the continued use of low-pressure haystack boilers and simple expansion machinery were most noteworthy, in strong contrast to the more modern boilers and compound engines then in vogue in the fleets of the Glasgow & South Western Railway and the Caledonian Steam Packet Company. Perfectly practical considerations, however, supported the Craigendoran management's loyalty to older forms of propulsion. North British steamers could be built at substantially lower cost than their competitors, and yet compete on equal terms at least as far as speed was concerned. They lasted quite as well as the more expensive vessels at Greenock and Gourock and North British policy can be seen in retrospect to have been more rational than that of their rivals, whose resources were lavished upon magnificent ships which failed to develop traffic to a profitable level and became simply a financial drain.

Changes at Craigendoran

By the late nineties, Clyde excursion traffic, as distinct from regular services, was growing to such an extent that the North British manager, Robert Darling, apparently felt it desirable to experiment tentatively in that field. The steamer *Redgauntlet*, built for the Rothesay service in 1895, was fitted out with a dining saloon on the main deck and otherwise modified to undertake a new daily excursion from Craigendoran round the island of Bute, commencing in the summer of 1898. The results were so encouraging that the construction of a much larger vessel, designed principally to expand the company's excursion trade, was discussed by the directors, and late in September of the same year Robert Darling was instructed to 'draw a specification of a new and improved steamer that would be suitable both for the ordinary Clyde traffic in connection with North British Railway trains, and for excursion traffic'.

Five leading firms of shipbuilders were invited to tender for a steamer on the basis of Darling's specification, but three declined to do so. The Clydebank Shipbuilding & Engineering Co Ltd, successors to J. & G. Thomson, offered to build the vessel for £23,300, while A. & J. Inglis of Pointhouse offered to build either according to specification for the sum of £23,950, or to produce a steamer five feet longer for £24,200. These tenders were considered by the company at a meeting on 20 October 1898, when 'after consideration it was resolved to accept Messrs. A. & J. Inglis' offer of £24,200 for a Steamer 235 feet by 26 feet by eight feet six inches moulded depth, with compound diagonal Engines and 'Haystack' Water-tube boiler to give 2,300 indicated horse power, and the Secretary was authorised to conclude with Messrs Inglis accordingly'.

The new steamer differed markedly from her immediate predecessors, the identical sisters *Kenilworth* and *Talisman*. Twenty feet longer than those vessels, and proportionately broader, she was the first Craigendoran steamer to have the fore-saloon built to the full width of the hull, so dispensing with the old-fashioned main-deck alleyways. The saloon was also carried forward of the mainmast, giving vastly improved accommodation for steerage passengers, but the promenade deck was not carried right forward and the bow plated up to that level

The Bristol Channel steamer *Lorna Doone* on trials on the Clyde when new in 1891. In later years this favourite steamer became best known on the south coast in radically altered form, but in her original state, as seen here, she bore a marked resemblance to the Glasgow & South Western paddle steamer *Neptune. G. E. Langmuir Collection*

The Glasgow & South Western Railway steamer *Neptune* in Rothesay Bay. She is in her original condition in this photograph, but in later years was altered by the addition of steel plating round the forward end of the sponsons and saloon and the addition of an enlarged deckhouse on the promenade deck. *G. E. Langmuir Collection*

The Craigendoran steamer *Waverley* approaching Rothesay. She is seen here in her final structural condition, as sailing from 1933 to 1935, but the old North British colours were abandoned in favour of grey hull and white saloons in 1936, and it was in that livery the *Waverley* ended her Clyde career. *John Crosby Collection*

The *Neptune* as she appeared after her reconstruction in 1912. Note the steel plating on saloon and paddle wings, the additional lifeboat at her stern, and the extended deckhouse on the promenade deck. *G. E. Langmuir Collection*

as had become standard practice in the Glasgow & South Western fleet by that date. Although there is no evidence on this point, one conjectures that the improved saloon had been suggested by the shipbuilders, an additional five feet being added to the hull length to maintain the required speed without an increase in engine power.

Unquestionably the most important advance lay in the machinery installation of the new ship which, for the first time in North British history, was of compound type. A. & J. Inglis fitted a powerful, twin crank engine typical of their practice, supplied with steam by a high-pressure haystack boiler. The combination was a novelty for Clyde service, although Hutson & Sons of Kelvinhaugh had first employed it on P. & A. Campbell's *Westward Ho* for the Bristol Channel passenger trade five years earlier. The haystack boiler had fallen somewhat out of favour towards the end of the century, being regarded as unsuitable for the higher working pressures required for compound and triple expansion machinery but, as already noted, Hutson & Sons and A. & J. Inglis developed improved haystack designs which came back into favour for several years. The haystack had useful advantages which amply justified its employment in the new North British flagship. Not least of these was its lightness; weighing only some fifty tons, the boiler had generous heating surface, allowing rapid steam generation. Sailing as she did in the shallow waters around Craigendoran, it was essential that the ship's draught be kept to a minimum, and for that reason alone a haystack boiler was preferred to the navy or Scotch types. Natural draught was relied upon for the furnaces, requiring the characteristic group of four large ventilators round the funnel, and it was observed that the vessel steamed best when sailing into a breeze.

The North British Company had favoured low-pressure boilers and simple expansion engines for so long that its conversion to compound machinery appeared as something of a *volte face*; it certainly drew ironic comment from Captain James Williamson, the Caledonian manager, who congratulated the North British for its 'courage' in taking a step forward. Nevertheless, the policy was quite sound. Compounding was undoubtedly more efficient, but its initial cost was higher than that of a single diagonal installation and probably outweighed any saving of fuel in service compared with the older form of engine. Steam coal in those days was so cheap that the North British managers could hardly have been unduly influenced by this consideration. One may wonder, then, what led them to adopt compound propulsion.

The answer almost certainly lay in the size of their new steamer and the duties for which she was designed. A large vessel of her class would have required a colossal single engine embodying the traditional disadvantage of its type writ large, namely the surging motion caused by unbalanced fore and aft movement of the piston and connecting rod. On long distance cruising this would have been quite unacceptable to passengers and it may be assumed that this factor, coupled with the need for increased power and speed, influenced the company in its decision to adopt the compound engine.

Trials and Service

At the *Waverley*'s launch on 30 May 1899 there appears to have been no formal ceremony. Robert Darling was gravely ill and in fact died on the following day. Secretary of the North British Steam Packet Company since its formation in 1866 and also manager from 1874, his had been a dominating influence on affairs at Craigendoran and it was the cruellest ill-fortune that he did not live to see his masterpiece, the new *Waverley*, in service. Her name might have been thought a natural choice for a company whose ships were named after characters in the novels of Sir Walter Scott and, indeed, an earlier ship had borne it, although not in Clyde service. (It was a ship built for the NBR Irish sea services out of Silloth.) The Campbells had a steamer built for their Kilmun trade in 1885 which took the name *Waverley*, but her departure to the Bristol Channel two years later left the opportunity for a North British ship to assume the title and it is strange that this apparently obvious choice should have been deferred until the close of the century. It was entirely appropriate for a vessel of such importance. The *Waverley* was in every sense a magnificent ship, beautiful, fast, and well appointed. Somehow the increase in dimensions compared with her predecessors in the Craigendoran fleet endowed her with greater 'presence', and she was beyond question one of the finest steamers on the firth. A. & J. Inglis had developed their 'house style' in paddle steamers by the turn of the century and the *Waverley* represented the pinnacle of aesthetic achievement for the Pointhouse firm.

Paddle-steamer design is very much a matter of individual taste and preference, but the construction of another celebrated vessel by the same builders within but a year or two of the *Waverley* showed how alterations could reduce a beautiful ship to something much less attractive. The *Majestic*, built for the south coast services of Cosens & Co in 1901, was modelled on the Scottish steamer, differing from her mainly in the substitution of triple expansion machinery for compound, and by the extension of the promenade deck to the bow, with topside plating; while for open sea conditions in the English Channel, portholes replaced the fore-saloon windows. The *Majestic* was a successful and well-liked steamer, not unattractive in appearance, but in her case the proportions were marred by placing the navigating bridge behind the funnel. The unrelieved expanse of topside plating seemed to call for a forward position, whereas in the *Waverley* a low bow and short saloon were appropriate to a steamer with her bridge in the traditional place aft.

The new North British flagship went on trials with a party of guests on Saturday 8 July, running the measured mile off Skelmorlie at the very high speed of 19.73 knots, handsomely exceeding the 18 knots guaranteed by her builders and placing herself amongst the fastest of all the river steamers. Only the *Juno* and *Glen Sannox* of the Glasgow & South Western fleet could rival her and, as both were usually to be encountered on the lower reaches, the *Waverley* had really no equal on the upper firth. Robert Darling's recent death clouded the occasion but the cruise was continued round the island of Bute, the route for which the vessel had been designed, and the customary after dinner speeches formally marked the directors' satisfaction with the performance of their fine new steamer. Under Captain Malcolm Gillies, the *Waverley* took up regular sailings two days later, fitting in a return run to Rothesay in the morning before taking the Round Bute Cruise in the afternoon in connection with the 11.35am train from Glasgow (Queen Street). She was also much in demand for other cruises in her early years and became an immediate favourite.

The North British Steam Packet Company was finally dissolved and the Craigendoran steamers were transferred to direct ownership and control of the parent railway company during the autumn of 1902. The only visible change was the appearance of a new pennant at the masthead, the St Andrew's cross on a shield being replaced by a thistle device on a white circle, the background remaining red as previously. The steamers sailed thenceforth within shorter limits, as the railway company's operating powers did not allow sailing to ports in Kintyre, Loch Fyne and the west of Arran, although the *Waverley*'s popular Round Bute Cruise remained in the timetables. No doubt the North British Railway, always more conservative and less willing to pour money into Clyde steamer services than its competitors, decided to economise by concentrating resources on the 'bread and butter' routes rather than on prestige cruises which often tied up expensive steamers for whole days on end with uneconomical complements. Increasing costs eventually forced the other railways to follow the North British example, and in the light of later events it is clear that the company's policy was more businesslike and realistic than that of others who competed so recklessly for coast traffic in the early years of this century.

The start of World War I in 1914 brought about an immediate curtailment of Clyde steamer services, and the anti-submarine boom from Dunoon to the Cloch, dividing the firth into two sectors for operating purposes, enforced a rationalisation of railway sailings under government direction for the duration of hostilities. The *Waverley* herself, like many other good Clyde vessels, was taken over in 1915 and adapted for open sea work by the extension of her deck forward and plating up the bow. Leaving the Clyde in November, she worked mainly from east coast bases throughout the war, but also saw service on the south coast of England as well as in Belgian waters.

She was discharged from Admiralty service in April 1919 and spent the remainder of that year and the first half of 1920 undergoing thorough renovation and improvement. It was decided not to cut back the promenade deck to its former position but to leave the bow plated up as in naval condition, and the bridge was moved from between the paddle boxes to a position ahead of the funnel. The result was to produce a vessel of fine, modern appearance in the general style of Glasgow & South Western Railway paddle steamers, but from the point of view of performance the outcome can only be described as disastrous. Mr. E. C. B. Thornton has pointed out the tendency of a paddle steamer to push her bows down when running at speed, unlike a screw vessel in which the effect is precisely opposite. The *Waverley*'s alterations so disturbed her original trim and aggravated this tendency as to reduce maximum speed by about 2 knots, while in the case of her consort, the *Marmion*, similarly altered at this time, the effect was so bad that she had to be withdrawn from service after a single post-war season and did not resume sailing again until the forward saloon had been cut back even beyond the original profile. The *Waverley*, however, was not altered again, and her impaired speed was apparently considered adequate for the easier schedules of the post-war period which were planned more rationally than those of earlier years.

The government offered compensation of £4,000 in respect of boiler wear and tear during the *Waverley*'s period of war service, and it was decided to put the money towards the purchase of a new haystack boiler which A. & J. Inglis Ltd agreed to install at a cost of £6,190. A new funnel was also fitted for £340, incorporating the unusual feature, for a Scottish steamer, of a navy cowl. Such provision was by then standard practice in the Bristol Channel and south coast steamers of P. & A. Campbell Ltd, effectively preventing smoke discolouration of their all-white funnels; but when there was a deep black top, as in the case of the *Waverley*, the fitting appeared superfluous and unsightly and it was removed after a couple of seasons.

Between the Wars

The *Waverley*'s reconstruction was finished by the end of June 1920 and it was duly reported to the board that she had been formally accepted from the Admiralty on 9 July. She immediately took up the popular Arrochar and Lochgoil service, with morning and evening runs to Rothesay, on which duties she generally remained for the rest of her career.

In 1923, the merging of British railway companies into four large groups followed the terms of the Transport Act 1921. For the North British as well as the other Scottish lines, it meant loss of their identities in less personal organisations and inevitable surrender of policy control to London. The change was symbolised for the Caledonian and Glasgow & South Western steamers by their appearance in new colours but happily the London & North Eastern Railway, of which the North British became the principal Scottish constituent, elected to retain for the Craigendoran ships their very attractive colours, although substituting a new house flag for the pennant of the old company.

The *Waverley* remained as flagship of the fleet until 1931 when she gave place to the new *Jeanie Deans* which, for that season, took over the Loch Long and Loch Goil sailings and released the older ship for work in the lower firth. When the *Jeanie Deans* took up her programme of cruises in the following summer, however, the *Waverley* returned to her usual haunts where she remained undisturbed thereafter.

In 1933 she was given a second major renovation in order to bring her standards of accommodation into line with those of the *Jeanie Deans*. The marine superintendent had submitted proposals to the Steamships Committee late in 1932, recommending the provision of shelters on the promenade deck, as well as alterations to the main saloon. The work was carried out by A. & J. Inglis Ltd at a cost of £2,288. Below decks, the old first-class saloon was remodelled as a modern lounge and part was converted into a tearoom, while, on the promenade deck, observation shelters afforded a much needed measure of protection from the weather. There was no question that the steamer was much improved from the passengers' point of view. The long, open decks of older excursion paddle steamers gave no shelter, and the excellent cover provided in the modern turbine steamers only emphasized the inadequacy of pre-1914 standards. Nevertheless, the cost to the *Waverley* was a further decrease in speed, and she was by this time far from being the record breaker of former years. Her appearance had also been affected, but the new steel deck shelters were grained and varnished to resemble teak and were relatively unobtrusive. In her modernised condition she was still a handsome and imposing steamer and remained a firm favourite on the Arrochar route.

In 1936 the *Waverley*, in common with her Craigendoran

consorts such as the *Lucy Ashton,* appeared in the new livery adopted by her owners partly to modernise the fleet's image but also to economise on the cost of annual repainting. The old North British colours were rich and beautiful, but the work of gilding hull and paddle boxes was undoubtedly expensive. The new, much plainer scheme – hull and paddle boxes grey, saloons and deckhouses white, and hull decoration largely abandoned – never became popular. Happily her distinctive Craigendoran funnel was maintained.

Finished with Engines

Due to falling traffic in the later thirties the London & North Eastern management effected sweeping economies in their coast services. Withdrawal of the *Kenilworth* after the 1937 season brought about a reallocation of duties, the *Jeanie Deans* going to the Loch Long route and the *Waverley* to the Rothesay and Kyles of Bute service for her final Clyde season. Thereafter she was laid up in Bowling Harbour during 1939, and it was generally accepted that her race was run. It was the last pre-war summer, heavy with foreboding of the world conflict that now seemed inevitable and Clyde sailings, amongst much else, continued in an atmosphere of unreality.

With the outbreak of war on 3 September came immediate resumption of the controls and curtailment of services which had been thankfully abandoned twenty years earlier. Air raids were expected to be a dominating factor in World War II and in anticipation of heavy attacks a large-scale evacuation of children from British cities was immediately undertaken. The *Waverley* was therefore brought back into service to carry Glasgow families to Clyde coast areas, and on completion of these duties was requisitioned by the Admiralty for minesweeping work for the second time in her life. She was based at Harwich as a member of the 12th Minesweeping Flotilla.

During the evacuation of the British Expeditionary Force from France in May 1940, every available ship was pressed into service to take off troops from the shallow, shelving, sandy beaches of Dunkirk. Amongst the makeshift fleet thus assembled were many paddle steamers, including the *Waverley*; and on 29 May she took aboard a full complement of battle-weary men and set off for England under heavy and continuous air attack. By skilful avoiding manoeuvres she remained undamaged for over two hours, zigzagging to escape bombs, while herself accounting for an enemy aircraft shot down by the anti-aircraft gun fitted on her fore-deck. Eventually, however, her rudder was damaged by a bomb which exploded close by. No longer under control, she was an easy prey, and in due course was hit amidships, sinking soon afterwards with heavy loss of life. So, gallantly, ended the career of the one-time pride of Craigendoran in circumstances which none could have dreamed of in the spacious and happier Victorian days when she first ran down river from Pointhouse as the new North British flagship.

The proud memory of this most popular of Clyde passenger steamers was perpetuated after the war when her builders turned out a new paddle steamer, destined not only to be the last ever built for the Craigendoran route but also, by a wide margin, the last to sail on the Firth of Clyde. As the new vessel left the ways in October 1946, she had bestowed upon her the famous old name *Waverley*. Sadly the story of Clyde paddle steamers ends with her; but during her career in the twilight of excursion services on the firth, and since then as a welcome visitor to many other parts of Britain, she has kept alive the memory of her great predecessor, and on a brass plate prominently displayed on her deckhouse appears the following inscription:

This vessel replaces the Clyde steamer Waverley which was built in 1899, served as a minesweeper during the 1914–18 war, and was sunk by enemy action at Dunkirk in 1940.

9

DUCHESS OF FIFE

One of the later railway paddle steamers built for Clyde service was the *Duchess of Fife*, a general purpose vessel which joined the Caledonian Steam Packet Company's fleet in 1903. A synthesis of the most characteristic features of her owners' earlier ships, she was arguably the most beautiful steamer sailing from Gourock and Wemyss Bay and certainly successful beyond the expectations of her builders. A career of half a century, broken by two periods of war service, testified to the usefulness of a steamer which was always regarded as ideally suited for the railway connections for which she was intended, and whose attractive appearance served for so many years as a reminder that beauty and efficiency could be happily combined in paddle-steamer design.

The Wemyss Bay Route

Of the three Scottish railway companies operating steamers on the Firth of Clyde in the palmy days before World War I, the Caledonian was perhaps the favourite with the travelling public. Its affairs were conducted with a flair and panache that attracted substantial traffic, it enjoyed a well-deserved reputation for smartness and punctuality, and its stations and rolling stock were amongst the most attractive in Great Britain. Something of the railway's merits attached also to its marine counterpart – the Caledonian Steam Packet Company Ltd – which owned and sailed the Clyde steamers based on railheads at Gourock, Wemyss Bay and Ardrossan. From its formation in 1889 the high quality of service under the managership of Captain James Williamson had been a byword and the company's ships which, at the start, set new standards on the firth, were high in public esteem. Drawing on the parent company's financial resources, the Steam Packet Company ordered steamers with modern boilers and machinery, while passenger accommodation was always excellent. Thus equipped, the Caledonian rapidly established a dominant position in the Clyde trade, driving lesser owners out of business, but inevitably drawing upon itself competition from the other railways until at the beginning of the century the contest amongst them was at its very zenith.

The Wemyss Bay railway had always been potentially the fastest Caledonian route to the coast, combining a fairly long rail journey with short sea links to the island towns of Rothesay and Millport. Despite its obvious advantages, however, for various reasons it had never been properly exploited. When the route was opened in the 1860s, early steamboat services were bedevilled by over-ambitious plans and poor management, resulting in the eventual collapse of the steamer company. Experienced private owners thereafter provided an adequate service for twenty years until the formation of the Caledonian Steam Packet Company, but even in the nineties the Wemyss Bay line did not succeed in attracting to itself the proportion of traffic that might have been expected. Although operated by the Caledonian Railway, the Wemyss Bay branch from Port Glasgow was originally owned by an independent company and, until its absorption by the parent concern in 1890, the coast trains terminated in Glasgow's Bridge Street station, situated on the south bank of the river and most inconveniently placed in relation to the city centre. The line itself was severely graded and crossed the Renfrewshire hills entirely on single track, both of which factors caused delays at times of heavy traffic. Not least of all, the terminus at Wemyss Bay was dingy, cramped and quite inadequate for a growing coastal trade.

With characteristic energy the Caledonian Railway turned its attention to remedying these faults. Larger locomotives and improved rolling stock were built for the route during the late nineties, the task of doubling most of the railway was completed early in the new century, and a splendid new railhead was planned at Wemyss Bay. These works were finally finished at the end of 1903 and brought at last a full measure of popularity to the 'Cinderella' line.

New Tonnage

In 1902 additional accommodation was provided afloat in the form of the first steamer built for the Caledonian Steam Packet Company for seven years, the fleet's now recognizable house style being exemplified by the new *Duchess of Montrose*. Her graceful hull, with pronounced sheer, was set off to advantage by the attractive Caledonian livery; but unfortunately, infelicitous details marred the appearance of what should have been a very pretty little steamer. The boilers were of navy type, with uptakes into a single funnel which unavoidably had to be placed well forward. Had it been well raked and proportioned, this aesthetic defect would have been unobtrusive, but the *Duchess of Montrose*'s funnel was aggressively vertical and spoiled her good looks. Another unattractive feature was her unusually small paddle boxes, the new vessel having been designed with small wheels with a view to minimising wear and tear. The combined picture just failed to satisfy, yet with a little more attention to design detail she might well have been just as graceful as her quasi-sister ship, the *Duchess of Fife*, the subject of this chapter.

The Caledonian Steam Packet Company had gone to John Brown & Co Ltd at Clydebank for the *Duchess of Montrose*, and from their predecessors, J. & G. Thomson, it had taken delivery seven years earlier of the famous and beautiful *Duchess of Rothesay*. When a second new steamer was ordered for the burgeoning Wemyss Bay traffic, to be ready for the summer of 1903, it might have been thought that the Clydebank yard would provide the extra ship; but a surprise was in store. Consideration of an additional steamer was first mooted at a board meeting in September 1902 and in December 'Tenders were submitted for the proposed new steamer, and that of the Fairfield Shipbuilding & Engineering Co. accepted, viz. £20,500'.

The Govan shipbuilders had never built a vessel for the coast services, although their large paddle steamers for the Thames and cross-channel excursion trades were justly famous. The new Clyde steamer was another masterpiece. She was designed and built under supervision of the Fairfield Company's newly appointed naval architect, Percy Hillhouse, himself the son of a Caledonian Railway officer, and destined eventually to become Professor of Naval Architecture in the University of Glasgow.

Guided by Captain James Williamson's specification, and evidently taking the *Duchess of Montrose* as his model, he produced an exceptionally beautiful ship, incorporating all that steamer's good features but none of her faults. There was the same slim hull, with open bow, which was such an attractive feature of Caledonian vessels. And what youngster could resist the lure of the forepeak, whence he could look down on the feather of spray lifting from the stem as it sliced through the water, or listen to the rattle of the steam capstan under his very feet as the mooring ropes were dexterously handled from the open space below?

The *Duchess of Fife*'s paddle boxes were larger than those of her sister, much to her advantage. They were, in fact, her crowning glory: Caledonian steamers were celebrated for the beauty of the heraldic devices on their paddle boxes but amongst many fine examples the new steamer was outstanding. The boxes were gracefully curved forward and swept back aft, the outer

The paddle box of the *Duchess of Fife*

faces being formed of delicate lattice strips following the main contours. Round the upper edge of each box was a dark-blue name board with gilded letters; and the arms of the Duchess of Fife, which formed a centrepiece, were of course painted in appropriate heraldic colours. All in all the white paddle boxes, with their profusion of gilding and ornament, gave an impression of richness and dignity and complemented to perfection the elegant lines of the ship's hull.

The ugly vertical funnel of the *Duchess of Montrose* was fortunately not repeated on the *Duchess of Fife*, which had a well-raked funnel of good proportions. The top part above the stay ring was rather deep by normal standards, but it was not a noticeable blemish until painted black in later years. Two navy boilers were fitted and the funnel was therefore placed further forward than might have been thought ideal; but the *Duchess of Fife* was so perfectly proportioned that one was seldom aware of this very minor flaw. There was compensation, too, in the generous deck space just forward of the paddle boxes which resulted from this arrangement. Taken as a whole, this was one of the great designs of Clyde steamer history. Even in her old age after World War II, she was self-evidently a queen amongst a river fleet much reduced by wartime losses.

Captain James Williamson had always been a pioneer in the field of paddle machinery and most Caledonian steamers were built with compound engines, or were converted to that system in the case of bought-in tonnage. A stage further was the introduction of a triple expansion engine in the *Marchioness of Lorne*, a general purpose steamer built in 1891; but she was not the most sparkling member of the fleet and in the *Duchess of Rothesay*, of 1895, the company reverted to compound propulsion with great success. In the *Duchess of Montrose*, however, the triple engine was reintroduced and repeated in the case of the *Duchess of Fife*. The system employed was a patent of the Greenock marine engineers, Rankin & Blackmore, first used by them in the reconstructed machinery of a small coasting vessel some twenty years earlier. It consisted of a cleverly designed arrangement in which high-pressure cylinders were placed in line with the intermediate- and low-pressure cylinders so that the pistons drove in tandem on to a common piston rod. Several advantages were thereby secured. The main one was economy of space, for the machinery occupied no greater room than a conventional compound engine which it resembled closely in appearance from the usual vantage point in the engine-room alleyway.

There was also no doubt an economy in first cost, for the more usual kind of triple engine with three cranks requires three sets of connecting rods, crossheads and valve gear as well as a more expensive crankshaft. The *Duchess of Fife*'s engine incorporated an impulse valve, a device by which live steam from the boilers could be passed directly to the intermediate pressure receiver, effectively bypassing and isolating the high-pressure cylinders. In these circumstances the engine worked as a compound at greater power, admittedly tending to drain the boilers, but a useful advantage when running for piers and a rapid burst of speed was needed to pass a rival steamer.

The *Duchess of Fife* was launched on 9 May 1903. She was named after Princess Louise, the Princess Royal, on whose marriage in 1889 the new dukedom of Fife had been created by Queen Victoria. One month later, on 5 June, the new steamer ran her official trials on the firth and delighted all concerned in her construction by handsomely exceeding the contract speed of 16 knots. The mean of two runs between the Cloch and Cumbrae lights was no less than 17.55 knots, 'a result highly gratifying both to the builders and owners', as the correspondent of the *Marine Engineer* duly reported. It was in fact a remarkable improvement on the performance of the *Duchess of Montrose*, especially as that vessel had theoretically more powerful machinery. What seems to have happened is that the hull of the *Duchess of Fife* was so well designed that the bow wave rose perfectly into the paddle wheels when she was running at full speed, ensuring that the machinery worked at maximum efficiency. The additional speed was a welcome bonus for her owners, placing the *Duchess of Fife* in the same category as their larger paddle steamers for operational purposes, and adding to her all-round usefulness.

Captain John Buie commanded the *Duchess of Fife* in her early years when she ran on general railway services from Wemyss Bay and Gourock to Rothesay and the Kyles of Bute, rapidly establishing herself as a very popular member of the Caledonian fleet. No outstanding events are recorded from this period and the absence of incident betokened her steady reliability as an all-the-year-round ship. In 1913, in common with most other Clyde steamers, she was equipped with an extra lifeboat and additional livesaving equipment following the stricter Board of Trade requirements in the aftermath of the *Titanic* disaster of the previous year. The new boat was installed on the promenade deck aft, but did not noticeably alter the vessel's outline.

World War I and After

In the spring of 1916 the *Duchess of Fife* was requisitioned for naval work, in common with the majority of her contemporaries on the river, and as HMS *Duchess*, auxiliary minesweeper No 533, operated out of Grimsby and Dover for three years before being returned to her owners. She was reconditioned in time to resume her peacetime duties in the summer of 1919 but it was a sad homecoming to a reduced Caledonian fleet; her quasi-sister, the *Duchess of Montrose*, had been lost through striking a mine on war service and the old flagship, the *Duchess of Hamilton*, had met with a like fate. Also in 1919 came the death of Captain James Williamson, perhaps the greatest single figure in the whole history of Clyde steamer development, and so it was in new hands that the depleted fleet took up its work in a world very different from the spacious pre-war years.

Financial difficulties hitherto undreamed of brought about the radical regrouping of Britain's railway companies in 1923 and those time-honoured rivals, the Caledonian and Glasgow & South Western railways, were amalgamated with other English and Scottish companies to form the new London, Midland & Scottish Railway. As we have already seen, an unusual situation obtained thereafter on the Clyde. The Caledonian Steam Packet Company's ships enjoyed unlimited sailing rights on the firth but the steamers of the Glasgow & South Western fleet, under their new owners, continued to be restricted by the terms of the Act of Parliament which granted the original powers in 1891. They could not, for example, sail up river to Glasgow, nor go to Campbeltown or into Loch Fyne, calling at piers, although cruising into those waters was permitted provided no calls were made. The restrictions were inconvenient, but for the time being caused little trouble in the large combined fleet.

The *de facto* unity also made it expedient to standardise liveries and in 1923 a new colour was adopted for the funnels of all these vessels – yellow, with red band and black top. It was the livery of the Goole steamships of the Lancashire & Yorkshire Railway, also an LMS constituent, but the consensus in Scotland was that it represented an attempt to combine the basic elements of 'Caley' and 'Sou' West'. As with most compromises, it was ill-received by both factions, which continued to interpret matters

121

in their own way. Thus the Glasgow & South Western steamers sailed in 1923 with very broad funnel bands and retained their grey hulls, while the Caledonian ships had narrow bands and black tops on the funnels, but their elaborate saloon panelling was still in evidence. In the following season black hulls, with white saloons and paddle boxes, became universal, as did the narrow funnel bands; but the last feature was abandoned after 1924 and all steamers appeared thenceforth with yellow funnels with black tops.

The effect of the transitional colours on the *Duchess of Fife* was unfortunate, for her funnel stay ring was placed rather far down, so that the black top was very deep and this depth was accentuated by the red band. The result was disfiguring, and the new style quickly became known as 'the tartan funnel'. From 1925 the colour scheme was much improved, being fresh and even brilliant in fine weather, but it was rather funereal; the pink and blue panelled saloons of earlier days had varied the Caledonian colours, but all-white was too plain and the black funnel top looked 'heavy'. However, the beautiful paddle boxes were unchanged and the intricacy of their adornment remained as a colourful relic of pre-war days.

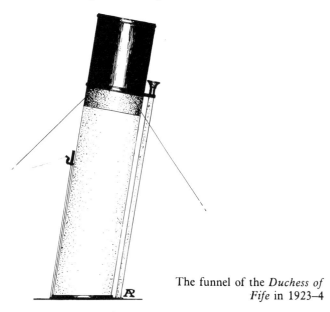

The funnel of the *Duchess of Fife* in 1923–4

The engine room of the *Duchess of Fife* in her early years, showing the elegant design of the twin crank, triple expansion Fairfield machinery. Note in particular the solid-forged crankshaft. *Author's Collection*

'The end of an auld sang' — the *Duchess of Fife* lying at Gourock Pier on Coronation Day, 1953 at the end of her Clyde service. Note the winter boarding round the saloon windows. *Photograph by the Author*

The Buchanan steamer *Eagle III* arriving at Rothesay during the inter-war period. She is in her rebuilt form with bridge forward of the funnel and painted in the colours of the combined Williamson-Buchanan fleet. *John Crosby Collection*

The Loch Lomond steamer *Prince Edward* approaching Tarbet in 1951. She is in the British Railways colours of 1949–52. Note the absence of a mast. *Dr J. Anthony Weir*

Peacetime Service

Essentially an economical all-the-year-round steamer, the *Duchess of Fife* was used constantly during the inter-war years, her vulnerable saloons and open bow being boarded up during the winter months as a protection against the heavy seas which sweep the Clyde estuary in bad weather. From a distance, while thus protected, the casual observer might easily have mistaken her for a steamer of the conventional plated bow type. She was usually employed on general railway connections from Gourock and Wemyss Bay throughout the twenties and early thirties, but became identified with no particular route. Probably the most useful member of the fleet, she combined economy with a good turn of speed and excellent carrying capacity and, although to some extent overshadowed by her larger consorts, was nevertheless a great favourite with the Glasgow crowds who had come to look upon her as one of the permanent features of their native firth.

In the summer of 1936 the even flow of her existence was enlivened by her being temporarily stranded at Kirn, but happily she was virtually undamaged and resumed her sailings almost at once. In the following year she began an association with the Wemyss Bay, Millport and Kilchattan Bay route which was destined to last for the remainder of her career. This is a delightful part of the firth, on which older steamers were often placed towards the end of their lives and it might well have been thought that the transfer of the *Duchess of Fife* to that station heralded her demise, more especially as five new paddle steamers had entered the railway fleet within the previous four years.

Another War

The *Duchess of Fife* had many years ahead of her, however. On the outbreak of World War II she was quickly requisitioned by the Admiralty for the second time in her career, becoming an auxiliary minesweeper based on Harwich in company with those other Clyde veterans, *Waverley, Marmion* and *Eagle III* and, like them, made several trips to Dunkirk in 1940 to assist in the evacuation from the French beaches. Surviving her dangerous sorties, she was later transferred to Port Edgar on the Firth of

Forth, where she served for the latter part of the war as a training ship. Alone of her requisitioned paddle contemporaries she returned to peacetime service on the Clyde, all the others having been lost by enemy action or broken up at the close of hostilities. The *Duchess of Fife*, herself considerably worn out during the war years, was taken to Lamont's shipyard at Port Glasgow early in 1946 and completely stripped down, substantial parts of her plating being wholly renewed and ribs replaced, while her boiler was given a major overhaul and the machinery thoroughly renovated.

Thus rejuvenated, the steamer returned to the Caledonian Steam Packet Company's fleet in the summer and resumed her connection with the Millport and Kilchattan Bay route, interspersed with weekend sailings to the Kyles of Bute and general work from Gourock and Wemyss Bay as required. In 1946–7 she sailed with an open bridge as before, but in her first season as a member of the nationalised British Railways fleet she appeared with a wheelhouse. This overdue improvement was made, it is understood, at the request of the National Union of Railwaymen of which, by chance of steamer history, the crew were members. Apart from this the *Duchess of Fife* changed little from her early condition, although her new funnel of 1946 had the stay ring at normal level so that the black top was much less obtrusive. In 1948 the broad white boot-topping of Caledonian days was finally given up in favour of a thin white division between black hull and red underbody just above the waterline, and the neat little Caledonian pennant was replaced by the British Railways flag, an object of no beauty. These changes aside, the ship sailed gracefully into old age, beyond any doubt the most beautiful Clyde steamer of the post-war era and a continuing reminder of the great years of the railway fleets.

Swan Song

I first saw the *Duchess of Fife* at Largs in the marvellous summer of 1947 and still recall the vivid impression the lovely old ship made upon me as she swept majestically into the pier. In my early teens my knowledge of the Clyde fleet was almost wholly confined to my favourite Craigendoran steamers and, until my encounter with the *Duchess of Fife* on that memorable day, I had

126

no idea that any Caledonian paddle steamer had survived the war. It was the start of a love affair that continued until the vessel went to the breakers and during those years there were many delectable sails to Millport and Kilchattan Bay. It is probably only the jaundiced recollection of middle age, but somehow the weather in those immediate post-war years seemed to be much finer than nowadays. Always, it appeared, one sailed south from Wemyss Bay along the Ayrshire coast in blinding sunshine. How well one recalls the hot, noisy engine room of the *Duchess*, the bright brass and steel of the machinery, the sight of the paddles turning in full view (for the watertight doors into the paddle boxes were often left open) and the aggressive clang of the bridge telegraph, while every now and again would come a burst of activity and noise from the steam steering-gear auxiliary engine. Truly a world to fascinate a boy who loved paddle steamers!

The welcome return of national prosperity following years of austerity brought an alarming decline in Clyde excursion traffic in the early 1950s as private ownership of motor cars became more common and people began to explore holiday haunts further from home. It was in fact the beginning of the end of the traditional Clyde steamer trade, but few foresaw the inevitability of its ultimate collapse. The fall in traffic demanded radical retrenchment and, in a planned programme of economies and curtailment of services, the remaining Clyde veterans were doomed to early withdrawal; while many of the less important coastal communities were to lose their piers.

The measures were too drastic for a public still steeped in earlier traditions and strong opposition resulted in modifications to the original scheme. Eventually, a quartet of small general purpose motor-screw vessels was introduced in 1953, designed to cope economically with the reduced services, and their arrival spelled the end of the *Duchess of Fife*'s long and useful career. She sailed throughout the winter of 1952–3 and was at last withdrawn early in the following June. For a day or two she lay at Gourock pier alongside the first of her successors, the contrast in size and appearance between old and new styles underlining the fall in standards from the Edwardian heyday of the Clyde railway fleets. The *Duchess of Fife*, a classical example of all that was best in that period, had sailed for exactly half a century.

10

EAGLE III

The contrast between the steamer now to be described and the Caledonian Company's *Duchess of Fife* affords a classic example of the difference between the standards of speed and comfort which the Clyde traffic of itself was able to support financially in its high noon, and the facilities provided by the railway companies in their expensive excursion steamers. The latter, attempting to foster and develop a trade which would eventually justify the lavish service provided from the early nineties, built large and costly ships which private owners could rarely match. The *Eagle III* was designed for the excursion trade from Glasgow, traditionally based on cheap fares, and few extravagances could be afforded in her construction and operation. Nevertheless, this 'plain Jane' became very popular on the firth and a reliable and useful member of the Clyde steamer fleet despite the most eventful early career of any modern paddle ship.

The Buchanan Fleet

When the Caledonian Railway, closely followed by its Glasgow & South Western rivals, successively entered the Clyde steamer trade towards the end of the nineteenth century, the old pattern of river steamboat ownership was swept away within a few years. Several privately owned fleets disappeared, either into the hands of the railway companies or by sale to other parts of Britain; the surviving ships of the mid-Victorian period were rebuilt to modern standards; and within a decade the Clyde boasted the most up to date fleet of its kind possibly in the world. The Buchanan family, whose connection with the river steamboat trade went back to the 1850s, were amongst the very few private owners who were able, by good fortune and careful management, to survive the revolution in coastal services.

During the eighties the family had a large fleet operating throughout the year on some of the most important routes on the firth, but on such services were quite unable to cope with railway opposition. The inadequacy of their *Scotia* on the Ardrossan–Arran service has already been noticed in the chapter dealing with the *Duchess of Hamilton*. Inevitably, there had to be retrenchment; and the Buchanans adopted a sensible policy of running economical steamers on popular routes at attractive fares, latterly in summer only. Thereby they retained a valuable connection particularly amongst the working people of Glasgow, whose loyalty to them remained constant for many years. Most of their ships were acquired second-hand, and several old favourites ended their days on Buchanan's up-river excursion services, amongst them North British steamers *Jeanie Deans* and *Guy Mannering*. Now and again a new ship was added, one of the best known being the Rutherglen-built *Isle of Arran* of 1892.

Broomielaw Sailings

Sailings 'doon the watter' from Glasgow fell into decline during the latter part of the nineteenth century mainly because of railway competition but also because of the dirty condition of the river itself. For years it had been treated as a convenient sewage system by a fast-growing city, so that by the eighties a trip from the Broomielaw could be something of an ordeal at certain times of the year. In hot weather the stench from the river could be detected well into the centre of the city, giving rise to a steady flow of correspondence in the local press. Complaints had no effect, warnings of epidemics went unheeded, and the citizens appeared generally resigned to a continuation of the unpleasant nuisance. Inevitably they deserted the up-river steamers in droves as soon as the new railway routes were opened, and in the circumstances it was a mystery that any of the Broomielaw services survived. Gradually, however, public opinion forced changes, the sewage problem was dealt with by a series of purification schemes, and by the end of the Edwardian period the Clyde had been restored to a state of reasonable cleanliness, if not to its pristine freshness.

With the improvement of the river came a revival of services from the Broomielaw during the first decade of the twentieth century. The Buchanans decided that the time was opportune to have a new vessel built for their own services, and placed an order for a paddle steamer with A. & J. Inglis Ltd in 1909. The Pointhouse builders sub-contracted the order for the hull to Napier & Miller Ltd, Old Kilpatrick, retaining for themselves the construction and installation of boiler and engine. Napier & Miller had been formed in 1898 to take over the shipyard and business of Napier, Shanks & Bell whose name we have already encountered in the building of the Glasgow & South Western steamer *Neptune*.

The nature of the traffic did not require a fast ship and expensive machinery could therefore be avoided. Nevertheless, the decision to fall back – for the last time in Clyde steamer history – upon the well-tried but obsolescent single diagonal engine in conjunction with a low-pressure haystack boiler caused surprise. The last example built for service on the firth had been the North British steamer *Kenilworth* in 1898, also by Inglis, and the new Buchanan vessel was a modernised version of that ship, being of the same length, but rather broader.

Built to Board of Trade No 3 certificate requirements for passenger excursion traffic, the new steamer however differed markedly in appearance from her Craigendoran prototype. The main alterations were the provision of a fore-saloon built out to the full width of the hull and the carrying of the promenade deck forward to the bow in the manner of Caledonian steamers. A feature of the Buchanan ships was a large awning above the top deck, abaft of the funnel, which was intended to be a floating raft in case of emergency; and the new steamer was duly equipped in this way. A practice which was distinctly old-fashioned by 1910 was the placing of the navigating bridge behind the funnel; it was the last time a new ship was so constructed, and retention of this outdated feature was possibly to minimise expensive modifications to the *Kenilworth* design.

At her launch by Mrs John C. Buchanan on 14 April 1910, the new steamer was christened *Eagle III*, reviving one of the most famous Clyde names of former years in conjunction with the very rare use of a numeral. The two earlier *Eagles*, both Buchanan-owned, had been built in 1851 and 1864; and since disposal of the latter in 1894 there had been no ship to continue the name in the family fleet. Trials were carried out satisfactorily in the early summer of 1910, when the steamer attained $16\frac{1}{2}$ knots on the measured mile. A party of invited guests enjoyed a sail to Lamlash, on the Isle of Arran, and as usual on such occasions were entertained to lunch on board. During the congratulatory speeches, Dr John Inglis of the builders proposed a toast to the *Eagle III* and her owners and made a number of well-received remarks about the anticipated success of the new ship, and after other speeches in similar vein the passengers returned to Glasgow, well pleased with their outing.

Trials and Tribulations

Previous Clyde steamer history offered no parallel to the sequence of events which soon followed. The *Eagle III* entered traffic in time for the Glasgow spring holiday and set off, as advertised, on her owners' popular excursion to Rothesay and Loch Striven with a crowd of passengers on board. The ship had not gone far down river however when, to the alarm of all, she suddenly lurched sharply and took up a permanent list to port, her sponson almost submerged and the paddle revolving in a torrent of water. The starboard wheel, on the other hand, was all but clear of the surface. Fortunately there was no panic, but the steamer was so manifestly unsteady that large numbers of the excursionists went ashore at the first opportunity, preferring safety to sorrow. The cruise was carried out as planned and repeated on two or three subsequent occasions, but the alarming list recurred whenever large numbers of people came aboard and, inevitably, the *Eagle III* was withdrawn from her station and moored in Bowling Bay until the cause of her unwelcome antics could be found and remedied.

Here was a problem for Dr Inglis and his colleagues at Pointhouse, for what more damaging advertisement could there have been for a shipyard than one of its new vessels behaving in such an unseemly manner! The *Eagle III* was brought up-river in the autumn of 1910 and slipped while her designers investigated the cause of her instability, which was eventually traced to the finely shaped hull. She was a 'crank' boat; and while some earlier Clyde passengers had occasionally been less than happy when crowded, the *Eagle III* was really unsafe. The cure was obvious, but drastic. The vessel had to be rebuilt to give greater beam, and this involved a major reconstruction. The first stage was to remove all plating from the midships section of the underbody. This done, every alternate frame was then removed and replaced by a new one of wider beam, which was riveted into place and, when these had been secured, the remaining frames were similarly replaced. The remodelled hull was then replated. The *Eagle III* had therefore undergone a unique rebuilding around herself, emerging apparently unchanged but rather beamier and, happily, no longer unfit for everyday service.

In March 1911 she was subjected to a series of inclining tests under Board of Trade supervision, as a result of which she was pronounced seaworthy and given a certificate increasing her passenger limit by sixty. The whole work was a technical tour de force on the part of the shipbuilders, but the complicated and expensive task of rebuilding the hull must have been a job which they were glad to forget as soon as possible.

'Plain Jane'

In comparison with the brightly coloured railway steamers of the pre-1914 era, the *Eagle III* was something of a puritan – a sober-looking little ship whose livery reflected accurately the nature of her owners' trade in which there was little room for expensive frills. She was the last new steamer to appear in the old Buchanan colours, the ancestry of which went far back into the first decade of Clyde steamboat history. The hull was black, with dark red underbody, and saloons were plain white. Paddle boxes were painted black in the first three seasons, but thereafter

The paddle box of the *Eagle III*

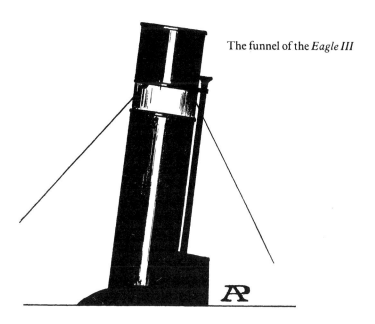

The funnel of the *Eagle III*

became white. Unlike the elaborately decorated boxes of the *Eagle III*'s railway contemporaries, they were simply designed with plain wooden slats separating the radial vents. The impression of austerity and even cheapness was relieved to some extent by gold lining on the hull and large, ornamental eagles as centrepieces on the paddle boxes. The black funnel, with a broad, white band, was the most venerable of all Clyde passenger-steamer colour schemes. It had been long established even when Captain William Buchanan and his partner, Captain Alexander Williamson, went into business in the 1850s and inherited the old Castle Company's funnel colours; thus when the *Eagle III* entered service, nobody living had known the Clyde without the black and white livery of the Buchanan up-river fleet.

Naval Service and Peacetime Success

When World War I brought an end to the familiar pattern of Clyde services the *Eagle III* continued to sail as previously, but the division of the firth by the anti-submarine boom from Dunoon to the Cloch and a steady reduction of facilities as steamers were requisitioned by the Admiralty foreshadowed even more radical curtailment as the world struggle entered its grimmest phase. In 1917 the turn came for the *Eagle III* to be taken into naval service and until 1919 she was used as a minesweeper in an auxiliary flotilla based on Grimsby.

When she returned, it was to a changed Clyde. Towards the close of the war years the Buchanan and Williamson fleets had amalgamated, resuming after many years the association of the original owners who had gone their separate ways in the early sixties. The combined company was named Williamson-Buchanan Steamers Limited, and into its fold came not only the Buchanan ships but all the paddle steamers of the Williamson concern – the latter's turbine vessels remaining in the associated company, Turbine Steamers Limited. All these ships adopted the plain white funnel with black top which was the hallmark of the Williamson fleet, and the old black funnel with its white band lapsed from use.

The *Eagle III* returned to the firth in 1919 not only in new garb but also structurally modified. When she went on Admiralty duties her bridge was moved forward of the funnel, and there it remained for the rest of her career. Gone was the characteristic Buchanan awning over the promenade deck and so, in rather different form the steamer took up her former station in the first post-war season, flying the star and crescent pennant of the Williamson fleet. For the best part of the succeeding twenty years she was to be one of the most popular summer excursion steamers on the river, regarded by the ordinary folk of Glasgow as quintessentially 'their' boat, sailing year-in, year-out from the heart of the city 'doon the watter' to Rothesay and the quiet waters of Loch Striven now, alas, all but unknown to a later generation. In the days before the motor car swept all before it, 'paw, maw and the weans' could board the plain, but smart, little paddle steamer at the Broomielaw and sail down past the famous shipyards of their native river to the enchantments of the firth beyond, enjoying not only the trip itself but also a good lunch and plain tea for a ludicrously low inclusive fare. There was probably no Clyde excursion steamer of her time which offered better value for money, and her bargain fares were a godsend to many a family in the black depression years of the thirties. Small wonder that the hard-worked little vessel was often remembered with more genuine affection than many of her grander railway contemporaries.

The *Eagle III*, like so many of her passengers, was a *worker*, and since her owners like them could ill afford to spend money unnecessarily, many of the trimmings regarded as a *sine qua non* on the better known river steamers were conspicuous by their absence in the Buchanan steamer. Nevertheless, unlike the latter, she was required to pay her way; and not until the difficult financial times of the mid-thirties did her owners find it impossible to carry on.

The *Eagle III*'s regular departure from Glasgow was at 11am and this was maintained until 1933 when she began sailing at the earlier hour of 9.30 to Rothesay only. Two years later, on 1 October 1935, she and all her sisters in the Williamson-Buchanan and Turbine steamer fleets passed into the ownership of the Caledonian Steam Packet Company Ltd, and although within a few months a new subsidiary concern – Williamson-Buchanan Steamers (1936) Ltd – was formed to take them over, rationalisation of the combined Clyde services began at once and brought the *Eagle III* on to the Glasgow and Lochgoilhead station during the summer of 1936. Despite the change of ownership the white funnel was retained, and when the steamer reverted to her old Rothesay route in 1937 it seemed to the general public that little had altered. However, for the little Buchanan steamer, as for many others in the Clyde fleets, time was running out as the European political scene darkened. The resurgence of Germany under Hitler was an increasing threat that could not be ignored and there can have been few people in Britain who were surprised at the outbreak of World War II in September 1939.

Under Fire

The *Eagle III*, along with most other Clyde steamers, was requisitioned early by the Admiralty for war work. She was taken over in October 1939 and converted for minesweeping duties, the main saloon being cut well back from the stern to make room for sweeping gear, while an anti-aircraft gun was mounted on the foredeck and her bright peacetime colours disappeared under a coat of naval grey. Thus modified, she was given the name *Oriole* to avoid duplication with another ship and, largely manned by her own crew but commanded by Royal

Naval Reserve officers, set off for Harwich to join a minesweeping flotilla otherwise composed of the LNER steamers *Waverley* and *Marmion* and the Caledonian *Duchess of Fife*. There, for four months, she patrolled the coast with that blend of tedious monotony and ever-present danger which was the characteristic lot of the minesweeper.

The pattern was interrupted dramatically on the fall of France in the early summer of 1940 and the evacuation from there of the British forces. On 28 May the Harwich minesweepers were despatched to Yarmouth for refuelling and sailed thence to La Paune, seven miles north of Dunkirk. The *Oriole* was commanded by Lieutenant E. L. Davies, with Sub Lieutenant J. R. Crosby RNVR, as first officer – the latter a young man of great ability who had exchanged his peacetime career as a Glasgow bookseller for all the uncertainties and perils of naval service in one of the Clyde steamers which had been so familiar to him in normal times. Sadly, he was to lose his life later in the war, but his written and photographic record of the Dunkirk evacuation was among the most outstanding of those days and has survived to recall the part played by both men and ships in that remarkable operation.

On arrival at La Paune the *Oriole* was ordered to disembark troops assembling on the long, gently sloping beach; but it was evident to Lieutenant Davies that the men, who were weighed down with weapons and equipment, would have great difficulty in reaching his ship along the lifelines, quite apart from the fact that the whole operation would be unacceptably slow and dangerous under frequent attacks from German bombers. Accordingly, in disregard of naval regulations as to hazarding his ship, he deliberately ran the *Oriole* onto the beach and by doing so converted her into a temporary landing stage from which it then became possible to load troops in large numbers onto smaller vessels, so allowing the entire process to be substantially accelerated. Naturally the stranded *Oriole*'s position was extremely vulnerable for several hours, and during one heavy aerial attack the Thames paddle steamer *Golden Eagle* was bombed and burned out close by, while it was about this time that the old Clyde favourite *Waverley* was sunk on her return to England, laden with troops. The *Oriole*, however, was fortunate and floated off in the early evening, almost unscathed, to return to Harwich with a full complement.

On 31 May and again on 1 and 2 June she returned to the beaches and the mole at Dunkirk to carry troops to Margate, on her last trip bringing several hundred French soldiers away. Again luck was with her and the *Oriole* survived these exciting days with no more than a few bullet holes and the odd scar from bomb splinters. Her contribution to the Dunkirk evacuation had been of unusual value, not only in bringing back so many troops herself, but also in helping to take off many hundreds more who might otherwise have been left ashore; but her captain and crew would certainly have denied that they had done any more than many others to achieve the army's survival. The bravery of her crew was however suitably acknowledged by the award of the Distinguished Service Cross to Lieutenant Davies, while Sub-Lieutenant Crosby was mentioned in despatches.

The remainder of the war was, by contrast, something of an anti-climax for the *Oriole*, which returned to minesweeping service out of Yarmouth for a long period and latterly was stationed in the Firth of Forth. Although tedious, the work which she performed was in every way as valuable as the hectic time at Dunkirk, although by no means as dramatic as that justly celebrated operation.

Epilogue

On a summer morning in 1946 I glanced from the window of a Gourock train while passing the shipbreaking yard of Smith & Houston at Port Glasgow, and my attention was caught by a down-at-heel paddle steamer obviously intended for demolition. It was difficult to recognize the once-smart pleasure boat under her dingy naval grey paint. Neglect was everywhere, from the tangle of wartime equipment strewing her decks to the damaged paddle boxes and battered sponsons which betokened the months of inactivity in which her Admiralty service had ended. It was the *Eagle III*, back from the war, luckier even so than some of her sisters of happier years – the *Kylemore* and *Marmion*, for instance, sunk on active service after long careers; or the nearly new *Mercury* and *Juno*, both lost before they had made their mark on the Clyde services. The *Eagle III* in fact came very close to resuming her career on the firth. Renovation was considered carefully and had it been possible to replace her worn-out boiler, the old ship would probably have been repaired and put back in service. But of all the shipbuilders and engineers on the river, not one could be found to construct, for an economical price, a last example of the famous haystack boiler which had made steam for so many well known Clyde ships of earlier years. And so the *Eagle III* made her last short voyage from the Holy Loch, where she had lain anchored since the end of the war, to the graveyard at Port Glasgow. Thus passed from the firth the last representative of the most typical Clyde passenger steamer of the Victorian and Edwardian eras.

11

PRINCE EDWARD

Although passenger steamships were operated from time to time on several of Scotland's inland waters, only Loch Lomond boasted a fleet of paddle steamers, the ancestry of which can be traced almost as far back as that of the Clyde ships themselves. Possibly the requirements of an expanding tourist trade and the proximity of Clyde shipyards combined to encourage early development of steam navigation on 'the Queen of Scottish Lakes', but whatever the reason the loch has known the beat of paddles for over a century and a half and now bids fair to see the last operating paddle steamer in the British Isles. Railway ownership came early, through acquisition by the North British Steam Packet Company of the ships and assets of the Lochlomond Steamboat Company in the autumn of 1888. Ruinous competition with the Caledonian Railway was fortunately avoided when the fleet was transferred to a joint committee of the two railways in 1896, along with the branch line between Dumbarton and the pier at Balloch, at the south end of Loch Lomond.

Difference of Opinion

Modernisation of the steamer fleet required the immediate attention of the Dumbarton & Balloch Joint Line Committee, for its two oldest ships, built in the early sixties, were obsolete and becoming unsafe to operate. The method of their replacement, however, brought the Caledonian and North British interests into conflict. The former company wanted to build steamers considerably larger than those already in service on the loch and proposed fitting modern boilers and compound engines, embodying these items in a design based on the Clyde steamer *Marchioness of Lorne*. The North British representatives, on the other hand, sought to enlarge and improve the existing type of Loch Lomond steamer which, with haystack boiler and simple expansion machinery, approximated closely to their own Clyde vessels. Their ideas were based on the *Empress*, built for the old Lochlomond Company in 1888.

Disagreement reached deadlock and the matter was referred to the standing arbiter, Sheriff Sir John Cheyne who, after taking evidence, gave his award in favour of the North British proposals on the grounds that the Caledonian steamers would have been too costly in view of the anticipated loch traffic of the immediate future. Accordingly, two sister ships, the *Prince George* and *Princess May*, were built by A. & J. Inglis at Pointhouse in 1898 and floated up the short river Leven from Dumbarton to Balloch in time to take up service in the following summer. Modelled on the *Empress*, they were slightly larger and had much improved passenger accommodation, but were fitted with the same type of double diagonal simple expansion machinery and low-pressure haystack boiler-installation which had been provided in their prototype. Both steamers enjoyed long careers on Loch Lomond, the *Princess May* surviving for well over half a century until her withdrawal in the coronation year of 1953.

Towards the end of the first decade of the twentieth century it was apparent that the oldest survivor of the Lochlomond Steamboat Company's fleet, *The Queen*, built in 1883, was in need of radical overhaul and renovation; but after considering a report on her condition the Joint Committee thought that the expense of repairs would be more economically invested in a new steamer. William Fraser, then at the end of his career as superintendent of steamboats, had definite ideas on what was required and prepared a detailed specification of a modern paddle steamer. This he submitted in June 1910 to Colonel John Denny, the principal Caledonian representative on the Joint Committee and himself a well known Dumbarton shipbuilder:

Dear Colonel Denny,
I have received your letter ... regarding new steamer for Loch Lomond, and note that building on the Loch is banned. It is a thousand pities & seems so strange that the opinion of those who do not know should prevail. I had given this matter very careful consideration last winter & prepared some general particulars of a steamer required for the service on Loch Lomond built at Balloch,

The *Prince Edward*
arriving at Tarbet in her
last season in service on
Loch Lomond. *Photograph
by the Author*

The top casing of the
Prince Edward's haystack
boiler. Note the
characteristic layout of the
ventilators, typical of so
many steamers of this type
utilising natural draught.
Note also the high
standard of maintenance of
the ship in her last year of
service. *Photograph by the
Author*

The Craigendoran flagship *Jeanie Deans* arriving at Arrochar while on cruising duties in the early 1930s. This was the condition in which she sailed from 1932 to 1935. *John Crosby Collection*

and alternatively built on the Clyde to go up the river Leven, & satisfied myself that a steamer 180' between perpendiculars, over all about 186', with a moulded breadth of 23', over all 42', with a similar draught to "Princess May", could quite well be dragged up the river.

I certainly would have no more of the haystack boiler in any form whatever, and . . . I propose a marine return tubular boiler having feed water surface heater. With a generous boiler of this description, fitted with the spark catcher, a great improvement would be made on the smoke nuisance, of which you yourself complained on several occasions . . .

Dr John Inglis however, a director of A. & J. Inglis Ltd and also of the North British Railway, was a man of forceful personality and had his own ideas on what kind of steamer might best be suited to the conditions on Loch Lomond. Colonel Denny passed Fraser's specification to him for comment and gradually a number of features were abandoned or modified to bring the proposed steamer into line with North British practice. The dimensions suggested by Fraser were altered to a length of 175ft and a breadth of 22ft which were regarded as being the largest size of steamer that could be taken up the Leven.

The Caledonian had at first been inclined to favour construction of a new ship on the loch at Balloch, but in the face of Dr Inglis's opposition they compromised on an enlarged *Prince George* which would be built in a Clyde yard to minimise first cost. Restriction on the length precluded the use of a modern boiler, largely on the grounds that it would have been too heavy, and in the event the well-tried haystack type was substituted in the specification, albeit in a modernised form to provide steam at higher pressure for a compound diagonal engine. Almost inevitably the order for construction was placed with A. & J. Inglis Ltd at a cost of £16,300, the builders undertaking to guarantee an average speed of $14\frac{1}{2}$ knots failing which the sum of £1,000 was to be deducted for each knot or part of a knot by which the trial speed fell short of guarantee.

The new steamer followed the general style of later Loch Lomond ships stemming from *The Queen* and the *Empress*. On her neat hull, quite short by contemporary Clyde standards, deck saloons were placed fore and aft extending the full width of the ship but the bow was left open to facilitate handling the steamer at piers. The funnel was placed close to the paddle boxes, giving a well balanced profile, while the navigating bridge was situated on top of the purser's office abaft the funnel. The close links between the shipbuilders and the North British Railway resulted in a marked family resemblance between Loch Lomond and Craigendoran steamers of the time, this being particularly strong in the case of the *Waverley* of 1899 and her smaller consort, the *Marmion,* which appeared from the Pointhouse yard in 1906. Both vessels were closely similar to the Loch Lomond twins of 1898 and their quasi-sister ship of 1910; the latter, in essentials, was really a scaled down version of the *Marmion* as originally built, save only that her bridge was forward of the funnel. Both ships embodied the characteristic Loch Lomond feature of a dining saloon on the main deck forward instead of on the lower deck aft, thus affording passengers a good view of the superb scenery as they dined.

The author has long held the view that these Inglis products for Loch Lomond were amongst the most beautifully designed paddle steamers which ever appeared from that, or any other, British shipyard. Like miniature works of art, they incorporated the very best features of their designers' skill and in the unusually attractive colour scheme of the Joint Committee's fleet made a perfect picture amidst the loch scenery.

Modern Machinery

Into the hull of the new steamer A. & J. Inglis Ltd fitted an elegant little compound engine, rather similar in appearance to the double diagonal machinery of the *Prince George* and her twin. There were really very few detail differences, but one which was apparent was the design of crank webs, made with cut-away sections on the inner faces in the new vessel in contrast to the reverse arrangement in her predecessors. Such changes were of no mechanical importance but connoisseurs of esoteric detail may find it intriguing to note that the little MacBrayne steamer *Mountaineer,* built at Pointhouse in the same year, had crank webs arranged as in the Loch Lomond steamers of 1898! Mechanically, the most important departure from earlier loch practice was the long overdue introduction of compounding in the 1910 ship and the substitution of a surface condenser for the old jet type to give improved vacuum and so increase the thermal efficiency of the engines.

A notable feature of machinery in the Loch Lomond fleet was its very fine finish and decoration; moving parts were machined bright and invariably kept highly polished, while the entablatures were painted in bright colours and panelled and lined in complex designs. The splash plates forward of the cranks were elaborately decorated, a feature which was retained to the end of the steamer's existence. In Clyde steamers, engine-room rails were usually of polished steel, but the new Inglis ship continued an earlier loch tradition of highly varnished wooden rails. It was possible to walk between the machinery and boiler spaces, something impossible in most Clyde steamers, thus obtaining an excellent and unusual view of the machinery in action.

The urgent necessity for saving weight in a vessel which was to be taken up the river Leven led, as we have seen, to the decision to rely again on the haystack form of boiler, and the same consideration lay behind the agreement to substitute wooden paddle floats for the steel ones in Fraser's original specification. Several modern paddle steamers equipped with haystack boilers were then sailing in other fleets, having either been built with closed stokeholds and the forced draught system or converted at a later stage; and North British conservatism as much as a desire to save unnecessary weight probably led to the decision to adhere to natural draught for the new Loch Lomond flagship, which carried the typical cluster of four large ventilators round the base of her funnel to ensure a good flow of air into the boiler room.

Progress at Pointhouse was badly delayed during the autumn of 1910 when a dispute arose as to wages, resulting in a lockout of members of the Boilermakers' Society for over three months. Further interruption was caused by a serious fire in the shipyard towards the end of the year, and in consequence of these unforeseen circumstances the Loch Lomond boat was not launched until 20 March 1911. The matter of a suitable name had, of course, arisen at an earlier stage, and the North British general manager had invited Dr John Inglis to suggest one. He replied early in January:

Dear Mr. Jackson,
I wish you a good New Year. As for the name of the new
Lochlomond steamer – don't you think we should keep it in the
family and call her Prince Edward?

Yours faithfully,
John Inglis.

Nomenclature of the fleet had settled into a standard form by
1911 and Dr Inglis was on traditional ground in suggesting yet
another in a sequence of royal names. The choice of *Prince
Edward*, the heir to the throne following the accession of his
father as King George V in the previous year, was appropriate
and popular. A surviving minute of the Joint Committee records
that in the event of failure to obtain the necessary permission to
use the name, the alternatives *Edward VII* and *Queen Mary* were
to be considered, but eventually the original choice was approved
and tastefully carved busts of the new Prince of Wales duly
appeared as centrepieces of the vessel's neatly designed paddle
boxes.

The colour scheme adopted for the steamers owned by the
Dumbarton & Balloch Joint Line Committee was one of the
most attractive ever devised for ships of their type. Those long-
time rivals, the North British and Caledonian railway
companies, settled any differences over the livery of their jointly
owned steamers by perpetuating the grey hulls of the
Lochlomond Steamboat Company and choosing a red funnel
with black top – thus producing something very close to the
Clyde colours of their mutual antagonist, the Glasgow & South
Western Railway! Above a rich pink underbody the hull, saloons,
sponsons and paddle boxes were painted an attractive shade of
French grey, relieved by pale-pink panelling round windows and
winghouses, and white washboards at deck level round the top of
the saloons. Deckhouses were varnished teak and so too was a
prominent beading running round the hull and sponsons at
main-deck level.

Ship in a Bottle

The new paddle steamer ran trials on the Clyde in an
uncompleted condition during the spring of 1911 and finally left

Pointhouse on 4 May to begin her passage of the river Leven to Balloch. In a vessel of her size the usual difficulties were magnified. On such occasions the builders always had to rely on a high water level in the Leven during flood conditions in Loch Lomond itself, but the natural corollary was that steamers had to battle against strong currents throughout the passage, their own engine power having to be supplemented by teams of horses and large numbers of men hauling on drag ropes. Road and railway bridges over the river formed special hazards, countered by the vessels proceeding without funnels, masts and deckhouses, but in extreme conditions it was always necessary to navigate with particular care to pass safely under these obstacles. Apart from these dangers, however, the curvature of the Leven presented special problems, for in one or two places it was so sharp that a ship's bow and stern were all but aground on one bank while its paddles simultaneously touched bottom on the other.

From the first it was questionable whether a steamer of the *Prince Edward*'s size could be taken through without incident and in fact she had only reached Kirkland, near Bonhill, on 8 May 1911 when the water level fell and left her stranded. Ingenious expedients were devised to raise her sufficiently to reach deeper water further up stream, involving in the first instance pontoons lashed to the hull and, as a more desperate remedy, the use of a railway bridge as the basis of a temporary dam; but the latter plan had to be hurriedly abandoned when the bridge shifted slightly. The North British Clyde steamer superintendent, now also in charge of affairs on Loch Lomond, had many misgivings about these attempts and eventually found it necessary to dissociate himself in writing from any responsibility, but it was soon admitted by all concerned that the *Prince Edward* was immovable and so she had to remain where she was for the rest of the summer and autumn. Not until 4 November, when the loch was again in flood during continuously rainy weather, was it found possible to make further progress, and the steamer at last entered Loch Lomond two days later. Reporting to his general manager on the completion of the work, the steamer superintendent wrote on 7 November:

On Saturday morning a start was made from Kirkland where the vessel had lain since May. For towing purposes two Traction

Engines were employed instead of horses, and which proved to be of the greatest possible service. Indeed had horses again been tried, I doubt if the vessel could have got into the Loch. I may say that although there were 11 inches more water in the river than on 8th May, when the vessel stopped at Kirkland, considerable difficulty was experienced in getting over Bonhill Ford. The vessel stuck and though the engines were put full speed astern it was 15 minutes before she cleared the bank. Again at the Black Rock about two hours were taken to get the vessel over the bank, and but for the fact that the water was rising all the time the vessel would not yet have been on the Loch.

It will be necessary to grant a gratuity to those engaged in the arduous work of taking the vessel up the Leven . . . During the gale on Sunday they had to get out additional moorings and stand by them all day to prevent any mishap. The work on Saturday, 4th current, while heavy for those men engaged on the deck especially at winch work, was comparatively light compared to the labours they underwent on 5th, 6th and 7th May, and on which dates the men wrought from daylight to dusk.

Having survived her eventful passage, the *Prince Edward* was rapidly completed at Balloch and put into condition for the summer season of 1912, being formally handed over by her builders on 4 July, when a party of railway directors and friends enjoyed a cruise on the loch.

Change on the Loch

It is astonishing to recall that in the years just before the outbreak of World War I, excursion traffic on Loch Lomond was sufficient to support four quite large passenger steamers. Apart from the charming village of Luss, then a popular holiday resort, the loch had no communities of any size and, except for some pier-to-pier traffic by local people, most of the considerable trade consisted of tourist traffic. Nevertheless, a daily service was given to every pier in winter as well as summer in those days, although the manifest unprofitability was to be recognized in 1914 by the purchase from London County Council of two very much smaller paddle vessels intended to undertake off-season duties. In summer, however, the *Prince Edward* fittingly took her place as the largest loch steamer on the route from Balloch to Ardlui, calling at all the intermediate piers.

Her coming, and the withdrawal of *The Queen*, emphasized the radical nature of the changes in the pattern of Loch Lomond services in a period of just under fifteen years. Instead of four rather small steamers, two of which were worn out, the Joint Committee now operated a quartet which collectively were well able to handle the burgeoning traffic and of which only the *Empress*, of the old fleet, survived from the late eighties. Gone for good were the quiet days of the Victorian period when the loch was virtually the exclusive preserve of the discerning few, when the Queen herself, the Prince of Wales, the Empress of the French and other notables, from time to time chartered one of the beautifully maintained tourist vessels of the old Lochlomond Company. Increased publicity, cheap fares and popular excursions from Lanarkshire rapidly swelled traffic after the opening of the Caledonian route to Dumbarton in 1896 and transfer of control to the Joint Committee. And however much the more conservative spirits might deplore the discovery of the 'bonnie banks' by unwashed multitudes from Glasgow, change there was going to be, and the *Prince Edward* was tangible proof of the fact.

Outbreak of World War I in August 1914 had an immediate effect on Loch Lomond traffic, which fell away to such an extent that the unfortunate catering lessee had to approach the Joint Committee cap in hand to request drastic revision of his contractual obligations. Reboilering of the *Empress* and the arrival of the two London steamers about this time created considerable over-capacity and some of the boats were laid up for varying periods, one of the new arrivals in fact never being used. The end of the war, however, brought a notable resurgence of trade, much of which was due to overseas troops visiting the loch before returning home.

Grouping of the major British railway companies into four new companies in 1923 brought no changes on Loch Lomond, where control of the Dumbarton & Balloch Joint Line Committee passed naturally to the successors of the North British and Caledonian railways. For the time being it was convenient not to disturb the *status quo* and steamboat liveries and the Joint Committee house flag remained unchanged. Nevertheless, in the face of growing road competition, the loch services suffered retrenchment. The *Empress* was laid aside permanently after 1925 and the *Princess May* employed for a long period as spare steamer, while the small London County vessel, the *Princess Patricia*, took up regular winter work to allow withdrawal of her larger consorts in the quieter months. Along with the *Prince George*, the *Prince Edward*, however, was regularly used as the main service steamer on the principal sailings, a role which she fulfilled for all but the last few months of her career.

In 1933 the two owning companies dissolved the Joint Committee and assumed direct control of the railway from Dumbarton to Balloch as well as the Loch Lomond steamers, and a further rearrangement of services allowed the scrapping of the long-unemployed *Empress*. The winter timetable was thereafter abandoned in the face of rising costs. The steamers continued to sail in their attractive colours although the old 'Joint' pennant went out of use. The *Prince Edward*, which lost her mast during the thirties, was no longer able to fly a flag of any description. The loss was probably due to rot in the wood, but in spite of the disfiguring effect no new mast was ever fitted.

World War II and After

The fleet was further reduced by the breaking up of the *Princess Patricia* in 1938 and the *Prince George* during World War II. The surviving ships were laid up for a time and used as accommodation for families who had lost their homes in the Clydeside air raids of 1941, but towards the end of the war a service was resumed by the *Prince Edward* and *Princess May*, both vessels being fully employed in the summer months. When the war ended this pattern was continued, and there came a welcome resurgence of excursion traffic, particularly in the very fine summer of 1947 when the reopening of the London & North Eastern Railway's Clyde sailings to Arrochar with the new paddle steamer *Waverley* permitted resumption of the popular Three Lochs Tour. This day excursion involved sailing from Craigendoran to Lochgoilhead and Arrochar, where passengers disembarked and crossed by road to Tarbet on Loch Lomond to join the steamer for the trip to Balloch, or the route could be reversed. With coast connections from Rothesay during the main holiday season, it was one of the most attractive tours of its kind and remained popular for years until the all-conquering motor car swept it, with the paddle steamers, into the limbo of things past.

The year 1948 brought into being the nationalised railway system and unified ownership of both Clyde and Loch Lomond steamers. While the former were almost immediately repainted in a common livery — virtually that of the Caledonian Steam Packet Company — the only change on Loch Lomond was to paint the ships' funnels yellow with black top, which did not go well with the grey hull and pink saloons. Not until the next season was the Clyde livery applied, when the *Prince Edward*'s hull became black and her saloons white. The latter were panelled in cream, as were the sponson houses, and the deckhouses remained varnished teak. The paddle boxes were black, with crest and decoration in red and cream. The overall effect was certainly striking, especially in those early years when the quality of the painting and general finish remained superb; but as in the case of the Glasgow & South Western Clyde steamers a quarter of a century before, the new colour scheme seemed rather funereal.

The early 1950s brought a situation akin to that prevailing on the loch half a century before, with both the *Prince Edward* and *Princess May* requiring replacement or renovation. The latter was a lovely little ship but it was clear that money spent on her improvement would be a poor investment due to her age and old-fashioned machinery. Traffic on Loch Lomond still appeared to have enough potential to justify building a new steamer and accordingly designs were drawn up for a modern paddle steamer, compound-engined, to be ready for service in the summer of 1952. After forty years, the risks of floating a new vessel up the river Leven were not to be entertained, and the ship, to be known as the *Maid of the Loch*, was therefore initially assembled at the A. & J. Inglis Pointhouse yard in Glasgow before being taken in sections to be reconstructed on the slipway at Balloch. Due to delays, the original date of completion had to be put back by a year, and the *Princess May* therefore enjoyed a respite in the 1952 season.

The *Prince Edward* was the subject of an interesting proposal at this time, when serious consideration was given to her thorough reconstruction and modernisation. A surviving drawing shows the steamer with the promenade deck and topside plating carried forward to the bow, the bridge placed forward of the funnel, and two masts and a second lifeboat added. The latter provision is a reminder that the Loch Lomond excursion steamers, due to the nature of their work, had been exempted from the full Board of Trade requirements for extra lifesaving equipment after 1912, and carried only one boat slung from davits over the stern. It is not known whether the plans for the *Prince Edward* were prepared as an alternative to the construction of a new steamer, but as the continuing employment of two ships on the loch appears to have been accepted until 1954, presumably the intention was to improve the older vessel's accommodation which by now fell far short of the standard set by the new *Maid of the Loch*. Whatever the motives, however, the changes were never carried out, and the *Prince Edward* sailed practically unaltered until withdrawal.

When the *Maid of the Loch* entered service in May 1953 the existing colours were abandoned in favour of a striking new all-white livery, with plain yellow funnel. The first intention had been to keep the black top, but a day or so prior to launching, this was changed. In keeping with the new arrangements the *Prince Edward* was slipped at Balloch and repainted in the new colours, which suited her slim lines admirably. Unfortunately the plain yellow funnel soon became discoloured with smoke and soot, and a half black top was painted on in mid-summer. The effect was surprisingly disfiguring, and within a week or two the logical decision was taken to restore the full black top, and in this condition the steamer finished her working life.

Unhappily, this event was not far off. Excursion traffic on Loch Lomond had begun to fall away in the early fifties, and in retrospect it is surprising that the decision to build a new steamer was implemented, for it soon became evident that one ship would be able to handle anticipated traffic on her own. The summer of 1954 was dull and rainy, the service was not well patronised and these factors, together with signs of trouble in the *Prince Edward*'s haystack boiler in the spring overhaul, combined to ensure her withdrawal at the end of the season. A good deal of attention had to be given to the boiler before it was certified fit for service in the last year, and in fact the steamer was a fortnight late in taking up her sailings. It was an unhappy note on which to end her career but the decision not to spend more money on her was well justified by subsequent events. Almost certainly a new boiler would have been required inviting the large-scale reconstruction already described, and doubtless the falling traffic returns prevented any serious attempt to keep the *Prince Edward* sailing. She lay at Balloch for a short time after withdrawal and was at last broken up on the slipway there, leaving the *Maid of the Loch* as the last survivor of a once numerous fleet and a long and notable tradition of steamboat operation on the 'Queen of Scottish lakes'.

12

JEANIE DEANS

Grouping of the railways of Great Britain into four large London-based companies in 1923 meant the disappearance of the old Scottish railways and the end of much that had been familiar in the world of transport. The Glasgow & South Western Railway was reluctantly amalgamated with its traditional rival, the Caledonian, and the Clyde steamer fleets of the two companies, while technically remaining under separate ownership, became for most practical purposes a combined fleet. After some early experiment their colours were changed and the ships sailed from 1925 with black hulls, white saloons and paddle boxes, and yellow funnels with black tops. Although not unattractive, the new livery suffered by comparison with the old, and became identified with increasingly remote and apparently unsympathetic control from south of the border. Services were rationalised and gradually the importance of the South Western railhead at Greenock diminished as services were concentrated on the Caledonian route to the coast through Gourock.

The Craigendoran fleet was more fortunate. The North British Railway became a constituent of the new London & North Eastern Railway and the old colours remained unaltered. The only sign of change in ownership was the replacement of the neat North British pennant by a form of the St Andrew's flag on which was superimposed a device with the initials LNER and, next to the hoist, a white shield bearing a thistle, representative of the Scottish shipping section of the newly amalgamated company. This apart, the Craigendoran route saw no immediate changes and for several years was allowed to go its own way.

The Lean Years

Towards the end of the 1920s the great trade depression hit the Clyde shipyards, bringing unemployment and a grey misery which is still recalled with bitterness by those who lived through

154

that time. Many firms were forced out of business and new construction dwindled to a mere trickle of tonnage. Against this grim background, the news that the London & North Eastern Railway had ordered a new paddle steamer for cruising work out of Craigendoran came as a small but welcome shaft of light in a period of economic gloom without parallel on the Clyde.

It was in June 1930 that the Steamships and Continental Traffic Committee of the LNER considered a proposal to build a large paddle steamer for Clyde service, based on a specification prepared earlier in the year. It recommended that several firms be invited to tender, quoting separate prices for a vessel with compound engines and one with triple expansion machinery, and that each builder be asked to submit alternative proposals for a steamer along the general lines of the company's specification, with the object of keeping down costs. Ten firms in fact were invited to tender, of which only four were on the Clyde, namely, John Brown & Co Ltd, Clydebank; Wm Denny & Bros, Dumbarton; Barclay, Curle & Co of Whiteinch; and A. & J. Inglis Ltd, Pointhouse. The other invitations went to builders on the east coast, ranging from the Caledon Shipbuilding & Engineering Co Ltd of Dundee to Earle's Shipbuilding & Engineering Co Ltd at Hull.

Within a month the question of machinery was firmly decided in favour of triple expansion but, surprisingly, none of the firms which had been formally requested to tender for the new steamer eventually obtained the contract to build her, the Steamships Committee deciding instead to accept an offer from the Fairfield Shipbuilding & Engineering Co Ltd of Govan, Glasgow:

To the Directors of the London & North Eastern Railway Company,

Gentlemen,
We beg to hand you plans for a steel paddle steamer fitted with Triple Expansion Engines for the LONDON & NORTH EASTERN RAILWAY COMPANY, and will construct the same and deliver it at Craigendoran, Helensburgh within six months from the date of your acceptance and in accordance with these plans and your Specifications, Contract Deed and General Conditions and our accompanying letter for the sum of £52,650 (Fifty Two Thousand Six Hundred and Fifty Pounds).

Yours etc.

The only previous ship built by the Fairfield Company for Clyde service had been the *Duchess of Fife* over twenty-five years before. She had a well deserved reputation as one of the most successful steamers on the firth and much public interest was taken in the new LNER steamer and its anticipated performance. The attitude of the men in the yard however was sardonic, even in the midst of the depression; long accustomed to working on warships and great liners, they said that they would soon be turning out boats for the Queen's Park pond!

Nearly twenty years had elapsed since a new paddle steamer had entered Clyde service in any fleet, the intervening period having been taken up with World War I and the ensuing years of reconstruction, so that the new vessel came as a relief to those who feared that this form of propulsion was obsolete. There was no reasonable alternative to its use, however, on account of the shallow water at Craigendoran pier which was no more than eight feet deep at low tide, preventing the regular employment of large screw vessels. Much satisfaction greeted the traditional outline of the new ship, which was seen to be in most respects a larger version of the modernised *Waverley*; but this was hardly surprising in view of the railway company's stipulation that constructional details were to be modelled on those of the older ship. The new steamer was 15ft longer and had 4ft more beam than the *Waverley* but otherwise resembled her closely, save only in that two funnels were provided instead of one. The promenade deck was carried forward to the bow, which was plated up in modern style, and standard North British paddle boxes were fitted, with eight radial vents and traditional ornamentation, including a carved bust of Jeanie Deans, the Scott heroine after whom the ship was named. The choice was a happy one, reviving the name of one of the most successful Craigendoran steamers of the nineteenth century, whose popularity was destined to be fully matched by her successor and namesake.

On-going Tradition

The *Jeanie Deans* was launched at Govan on 7 April 1931 by Miss Rhoda Whitelaw, daughter of the chairman of the London & North Eastern Railway, and the new ship was ready for trials just under seven weeks later. Although she was thought to look her best in the years immediately after World War II, nevertheless her original appearance was impressive, her short funnels and small cabins on the promenade deck making for a simple, clean profile according well with her reputation as a flyer. The *Jeanie Deans* was driven by the first set of conventional three crank, triple expansion machinery ever used in a Clyde passenger steamer, designed to give her a maximum speed of $18\frac{1}{2}$ knots. These engines were most impressive in action; beautifully designed, they had Stephenson link motion similar to that of the *Waverley*, with short eccentric rods, and the expansion links were therefore in full view of passengers standing in the engine-room alleyways. The paddle wheels were fitted with elm floats which, by this period, were regarded as unfashionable; but the company could advance cogent arguments (see page 176) for retaining them in preference to steel floats. Steam was supplied by a double-ended boiler, with uptakes into two rather squat funnels forward of the paddle boxes, giving the *Jeanie Deans* the distinction of being the first two-funnelled Clyde paddle steamer to enter service for nearly forty years – the first, in fact, since the *Glen Sannox* in 1892. Unlike that vessel and her two-funnelled contemporaries, the *Jeanie Deans* reverted to the outline of her forerunner at Craigendoran, the *Meg Merrilies*, with funnels forward instead of being placed fore and aft of the machinery space and so avoiding the inconvenience of double stokeholds.

During the initial design stages a number of points were raised by the Fairfield Company with a view to amending the railway specification. One of the most important involved the proposed substitution of a solid-forged crankshaft for the built-up type requested, and paddle wheels with seven instead of eight floats. But the owners were adamant and no changes were made. They felt it necessary to insist upon the heavier, built-up shaft in view of unsatisfactory experience of the solid-forged pattern elsewhere, and eight paddle floats were thought to give a better shock distribution on the wheels than seven. A more radical proposal, also declined, was to employ yellow pine instead of teak for the promenade deck and to omit roof panelling in the saloons to save weight and permit finer hull lines; this in turn would have allowed slightly less powerful machinery and a saving of about £1,000 in the contract price. Evidently the owners had set their face against economies of this kind in a vessel built to capture a large share of the Clyde excursion traffic, for they also declined to accept the builders' suggestion to finish the funnel casings with snap-headed rivets, insisting upon countersunk rivets on the grounds of better appearance.

We have already seen how the *Waverley* lost much of her speed after the promenade deck was extended and the bow plated-in after World War I, and when the *Jeanie Deans* entered service she was undoubtedly the faster vessel, designed to run regularly at full speed on long cruises out of Craigendoran in opposition to the Caledonian Steam Packet Company's new turbine steamer *Duchess of Montrose*, which had appeared in 1930. The *Jeanie Deans* was a splendid example of paddle-steamer design, and a logical development of the North British style rather than a new variation. This was emphasized by continued use of the old Craigendoran livery, even taken to extremes by painting false panelling on the steel sponson houses. All the richness of detail was continued as of old – gilding on hull, sponsons and paddle boxes; cream saloons and topside plating, white lifeboats and, crowning all, those supremely attractive red, white and black funnels.

Widespread publicity was arranged when the *Jeanie Deans* ran an official trip to Arrochar on 25 May 1931 'beneath an azure sky and a sun which blazed down on a smiling countryside' as the *Edinburgh Evening Dispatch* reported. She conveyed the railway company's principal officers and a large party of pressmen who 'wrote up' the new flagship in eulogistic terms. For Captain L. H. Gilchrist, the retiring marine superintendent, it was a sentimental occasion; for him, at the close of his career, the wheel had come full circle. He had been appointed secretary of the old North British Steam Packet Company in May 1899 as the then new *Waverley* joined the Craigendoran fleet and now, after three eventful decades, was on the point of retirement as her magnificent consort arrived upon the scene.

The *Jeanie Deans* became an instant favourite. Her rakish appearance was much admired and it was seen that conservatism had been successfully combined with a notable advance in the standard and taste of her internal appointments as compared with steamers of the pre-war years – one reporter going as far as to suggest that they were 'such as any newly wed bride might

Triple expansion — the impressive machinery of the *Jeanie Deans*. The engines of the *Bristol Queen* (1946) and *Waverley* (1947) were of very similar appearance. *Photograph by the Author*

The *Jeanie Deans* arriving at Dunoon in the final years of her Clyde career, in the colours of the Caledonian Steam Packet Company, but retaining LNER black paddleboxes. *The late J. M. D. Warren*

covet for her home'. The *West Coast Courier* noted the first-class saloon's 'seating in large bays of well upholstered spring cushioned seats . . . writing tables of chaste design, mirrors, clock, and barometer. Draped curtains at windows in sides and end together with carpet runners on the lino floor make this a charming apartment'. A tearoom was situated on the main deck at the forward end of the first-class saloon, panelled in light oak and macassar ebony in harmony with the main saloon itself. Small tables were provided for parties of four, at which light meals could be served if required, and the furnishings again included carpet runners and draped curtains. The first-class dining saloon was on the lower deck aft, below the main saloon, and could accommodate eighty-four people. Steerage accommodation, conventionally placed forward, was much plainer, with teak seats, and was 'well lighted by large rectangular windows'. In this the *Jeanie Deans* followed usual practice, and newspaper comment concentrated understandably on the taste and artistry of the first-class saloons, which met with general approval. As the *West Coast Courier* stated:

> Altogether the *Jeanie Deans* is a 'bonnie lassie' and one that will win the hearts of the great travelling public. We hope that she will have a great and successful future. We can think of no more charming company than this dainty little lady for a tour of the Clyde beauty spots, and once seen, we know she will have many admirers, despite her reputation for being fast!

The *Jeanie Deans* spent her first season on the Loch Long and Loch Goil station, connecting at Arrochar with the Loch Lomond service to Tarbet, and providing the Clyde part of the well known Three Lochs Tour. A late-afternoon return sailing from Craigendoran to Rothesay rounded off the day's programme. This was the *Waverley*'s regular duty, to which that steamer reverted in 1932, freeing the *Jeanie Deans* to take up a series of excursions from Craigendoran which found her on occasions as far afield as Ayr, Girvan and Whiting Bay; and these were continued until the late thirties. Before the summer of 1932, however, several important alterations had been made to the ship.

Early Improvements

Much trouble was experienced during the first season with soot and ashes falling on the promenade deck, possibly due to the crew's lack of familiarity with the forced draught system. All other Craigendoran steamers of the period had haystack boilers working under natural draught. Similar problems had afflicted the Caledonian Steam Packet Company many years earlier on the introduction of forced draught when, in extreme instances, the use of unnecessarily high air pressures in the stokehold caused live embers to fall on the ships' decks. The LNER marine superintendent felt that the difficulty in the *Jeanie Deans* could be resolved by two improvements and on 7 January 1932 the Steamships & Continental Traffic Committee minuted the submission of 'Memorandum by the Marine Superintendent, Southern Scottish Area, suggesting ... lengthening of the funnels by 5 feet and grit arresters fitted in each funnel to prevent the discharge of soot and grit. The cost is estimated at £420.' The Fairfield Company's tender for undertaking the work was accepted and the *Jeanie Deans* emerged in due course in rather different form. Despite the figure quoted in the minute,

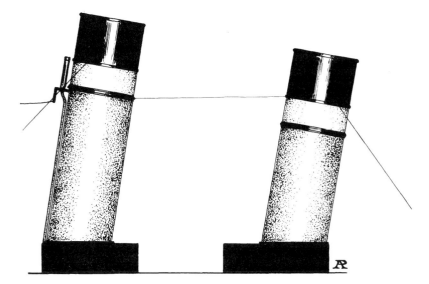

The stepped funnels of the *Jeanie Deans*, 1932–9

the fore funnel was lengthened by 9ft and the after one by 6ft. The effect of the alterations was reported as 'entirely satisfactory', although the visual effect of funnels of different heights was mildly bizarre from some angles.

About this period the company experimented with a device known as 'Neil's Rocker Firebar Grate' on board two of its Harwich cross channel steamers, the *Bruges* and the *Amsterdam*. Economy in coal consumption had been sufficiently marked to encourage the owners to equip other vessels too and the *Jeanie Deans* – the newest member of the Clyde fleet, and the only one with a modern boiler – was an obvious choice. A minute of the Steamships Committee, dated 28 April 1932, ran as follows:

P.S. Jeanie Deans. The terms of the trial would be that Messrs Neil Ltd. would guarantee a minimum reduction in fuel consumption of 7% over a three months' test, and the Railway Company on their part would undertake to purchase the equipment in the event of such a saving being actually obtained during the trial period. Subject to the firm's tender for equipping the six additional Harwich vessels being accepted, they are willing to offer the same terms for the suggested trial installations, viz., £45 per furnace, the fitting to be carried out at the expense of the Railway Company. Should, however, the guaranteed economy of 7% not be fully realised the Company would be under no obligation to purchase the equipment, and Messrs Neil Ltd. would be prepared to bear the cost incurred in fitting and removing their grates and replacing our own.

It was calculated that if the minimum saving in fuel were achieved, the estimated saving in cost of coal at pit price would amount to £59 over the trial period, on an outlay of £294, which was the expected cost of supplying and fitting the Neil Grates to the six furnaces of the *Jeanie Deans*. Permission to take up the Neil offer was granted and the equipment installed in time for the summer season of 1932. It was even more efficient than the manufacturers had anticipated, the saving in coal as compared with the first season amounting to .851 tons per 100 nautical miles, equivalent to a reduction of 9.4 per cent. An unforeseen additional advantage was a slight increase in average speed, while the reduction in coal consumption must in itself have gone a good way towards remedying the problem of soot and cinders.

A further improvement to the *Jeanie Deans* before she took up service in 1932 was the addition of a deck shelter at the forward end of the promenade deck. Provision for shelter had originally been negligible and in this respect the ship was really behind the times, as was plain when compared with the Caledonian turbine steamer *Duchess of Montrose*. The marine superintendent therefore proposed the provision of a light steel shelter with large observation windows, and the work was done at a cost of £414. The addition of this structure did not detract from the appearance of the *Jeanie Deans*; being painted and grained to resemble varnished teak it was unobtrusive. From the practical point of view, of course, it was an immense advantage. All in all, therefore, the *Jeanie Deans* began her second season as a much improved steamer – faster, cleaner, and more efficient than in her original condition.

Pre-war Service

The programme of day excursions combined with evening cruises continued season by season throughout the thirties with little apparent change at Craigendoran; but in 1936 the *Jeanie Deans*, in common with her consorts, appeared in the simplified grey and white colours which had so much altered the character of the *Waverley*, and it was not to her advantage. The new livery was not generally liked; it was cheaper to apply than the older colours which, of course, was the reason for its adoption, but it looked tawdry and unkempt by comparison with what had gone before. Unhappily, it heralded steady retrenchment in the coast services as the LNER cut back its Clyde commitments in the face of increasing losses. First to go was the *Kenilworth*, last survivor of the classic North British single diagonal steamers; she was broken up, unusually, by her original builders – A. & J. Inglis Ltd – in 1938, and not replaced. In the following year, the services were pared drastically when both the *Lucy Ashton* and *Waverley* were laid up pending final disposal, leaving only three steamers to maintain basic railway connections to the principal coast resorts.

The *Jeanie Deans* took over the Arrochar service, abandoning the long-distance cruises for which she had been designed. This and the more remunerative 'bread and butter' runs to Rothesay seemed to be her work for the foreseeable future, always provided that the LNER continued to operate Clyde steamer services at all. Rumours were rife during that season to the general effect that the company was about to dispose of its connection to the Caledonian Steam Packet Company, a move which, had it happened, would have brought about rationalisation of the Clyde steamer services a decade before state ownership took effect.

All such speculation ended however when Britain declared war on Germany on 3 September 1939 and the *Jeanie Deans*, in company with most of her contemporaries, was taken into Admiralty service. As in 1914–18, minesweeping was the main activity allotted to excursion paddle steamers and the *Jeanie Deans* was so employed during 1939–40. The threat of aerial attack on London and the Thames, however, saw the Craigendoran flagship's conversion to an anti-aircraft vessel in 1941, and it was in this capacity that she served throughout the rest of the war.

Indian Summer

In the spring of 1946 the *Jeanie Deans* returned to her native firth to resume peaceful activities. Gone were the depressing rumours of 1939 and there took place something of a revival at Craigendoran. The *Jeanie Deans* went first to A. & J. Inglis Ltd at Pointhouse to undergo a thorough reconstruction from which she emerged very nearly a new ship. The sight of this magnificent steamer being transformed into peacetime livery from dingy warship grey captured the author's boyhood imagination. Travelling to and from Glasgow daily across the Pointhouse railway viaducts, he saw the *Jeanie Deans* gradually being rebuilt into the most imposing paddle steamer he had ever seen. Remember that in 1946 the only paddle boats on the Clyde for several years had been the *Lucy Ashton* and the Caledonian *Marchioness of Lorne*, both small steamers, unimpressive in their naval grey. The sight of the gorgeously painted *Jeanie Deans*, so much larger than those two, came as a revelation.

Reconditioning for peacetime service resulted in radical changes in the ship's outline. The short quarter deck disappeared under an extended promenade deck and steel plating carried round the stern, while a section of the former open rail at the bow was replaced by plating. Capstan engines appeared at bow and stern on the promenade deck where, in pre-war years, only the capstan drums had been visible. The effect of these improvements was to release more comfortable accommodation for the crew, whose former accommodation had been spartan. A second deck shelter was added aft, of similar pattern to the one which had been placed on the fore-deck in 1932, giving much improved cover from rain and wind. The flying decks on both shelters were carried out to the ship's rail, serving the double purpose of supporting the four lifeboats and providing extra cover. The old 'swan neck' davits were replaced by new ones of Welin type, which were certainly more obtrusive than the originals but marked a considerable advance in standards of safety at sea. The open navigating bridge of the early years was replaced by a new one with wheelhouse and captain's cabin, the combined structure appearing as before on the flying deck above the forward shelter. The addition of a mainmast and substitution of large new funnels of equal height for the old 'joggled' ones gave an immensely improved profile, and in this condition few would have disputed that the *Jeanie Deans* looked her finest, for the funnels and superstructure of the thirties had really been out of proportion to the hull of this large, powerful steamer.

Internal renovation was comprehensive, involving a departure from the time-honoured Clyde arrangement of having the first-class saloon on the main deck aft with a dining saloon on the lower deck. Passengers could see nothing while dining, for the waterline portholes were simply to provide light and as often as not were awash. When the *Jeanie Deans* was altered, a well-equipped dining saloon was substituted for the first-class saloon on the main deck. It was by no means a novel feature – earlier Craigendoran steamers on the Arrochar service had been built with dining saloons on the main deck forward – but it was sufficiently rare to be welcomed as a notable improvement, allowing passengers to watch the scenery as they dined. A new first-class saloon was provided on the main deck forward of the boiler space and, although not large, it was comfortably furnished with armchairs and sofas and became a much sought-after haven in bad weather. The steerage accommodation was restricted to the deck shelters, but by 1946 the trend favoured by the public was firmly towards 'first class only', a tendency acknowledged by the abolition of class distinctions in the early 1950s.

The transformation of the LNER flagship was completed by a welcome return to the old North British colours which had been abandoned in 1936. The hull reverted to black, above a dark-red underbody, a thin white line dividing black from red at the waterline. Saloons and sponson houses were cream without the pseudo-panelling of the early years, this simplification enhancing the general effect. Deck saloons were grained and varnished to resemble the natural woodwork of bridge and wheelhouse, but the white boats and davits lightened what might otherwise have been a sombre colour scheme. The funnels were bright red, with broad white bands and black tops and – an important detail – black stay rings between red and white. The main change from older times lay in the substitution of yellow paint for gold in the lining and decoration of hull and paddle boxes, but there were few complaints on that score for the *Jeanie Deans* looked splendid in her new finery.

She ran trials on 15 June 1946 before taking up the principal Craigendoran–Rothesay runs, calling intermediately at Kilcreggan, Kirn, Dunoon, Innellan and Rothesay. She was a magnificent sight in that season; for all practical purposes a new steamer, and an absolute picture in her peacetime livery. Later in the summer she and the veteran *Lucy Ashton* were joined by the unique diesel-electric paddle vessel *Talisman* which had also been thoroughly reconditioned and improved after war service, and it became possible to extend LNER sailings to Auchenlochan in the western Kyles of Bute. The service to Arrochar, however, was not reinstated until the new *Waverley* came into the fleet in the early summer of 1947.

The year of the heatwave is how 1947 is still remembered, and in the transport sphere it symbolised the Indian summer of the Clyde steamers on the eve of nationalisation. For the last season the red, white and black funnels of the old North British Company were seen at Craigendoran where four berths could again be filled of a summer evening. Picture a twilight in that perfect summer, the firth calm under a glowing sunset, and the four LNER paddle vessels moored side by side at the pier – the *Lucy Ashton*, oldest of the whole Clyde fleet, and a tangible reminder not only of the great days before World War I but also of the older steamers of Queen Victoria's time; the *Waverley*, inheritor of a proud name and tradition, and youngest and last of the Craigendoran family; the *Talisman*, odd ship of the fleet in many respects but now accepted by all as a worthy member; and, lying in the principal berth, the flagship, the rejuvenated *Jeanie Deans*.

State Ownership

In 1948 came nationalisation of the railways and unification of the Clyde fleets. Early in the year it was announced that liveries would be standardised, and the bright funnels of Craigendoran disappeared at last under the buff and black of British Railways; for the new administration assumed direct control of the ships, dispensing with the old LMS subsidiary, the Caledonian Steam Packet Company. The *Jeanie Deans* and her sisters had the saloons painted white in accordance with Gourock practice, and all ships now wore a new flag – an unhappy, cluttered thing bearing the lion and wheel emblem of the state transport system.

For the time being, however, certain Craigendoran features remained, such as varnished teak finish for the observation saloons on the promenade deck – these were white on the Gourock steamers – and black paddle boxes with appropriate decoration. In practice the 1948 season saw little change and the LNER fleet maintained broadly similar services until the end of the forties. But with the harsher financial climate of the ensuing decade came radical changes in the entire Clyde service as increasing running costs and falling traffic caused such losses that drastic reductions in services and withdrawal of older steamers were suggested, along with wholesale pier closures. An immediate public outcry led to eventual revision and compromise, involving the building of four small passenger ships in 1953, and these, along with a dwindling number of excursion steamers, maintained an annual programme into the seventies.

The *Jeanie Deans* was subjected to detail alterations during the next fifteen years. Her deck shelters became white eventually, but unlike her consorts *Talisman* and *Waverley* she retained black paddle boxes until withdrawal. When ownership of the Clyde steamers was transferred to a resuscitated

Caledonian Steam Packet Company in 1954 the neat pennant with lion rampant replaced the unattractive banner of British Railways. Another change, much less happy, was the dropping of hull lining about this period. Its omission from the plainer hulls of turbine steamers had been standard practice from the first, but the removal of lining from paddle steamers detracted considerably from their appearance.

The *Jeanie Deans* settled into a routine on the favourite Craigendoran cruise to Rothesay and round the island of Bute, varying this by Sunday cruises to Skipness and occasional forays to Arrochar where the author recalls her, appropriately dressed overall, on Coronation Day, in June 1953. Latterly she and the *Waverley* alternated week about on Craigendoran sailing rosters and the *Jeanie Deans* in her last years could be seen all over the firth, as far south as Pladda on occasions. She remained to the end an imposing steamer, well maintained and a general favourite. By 1964 she was no great age by Clyde standards, especially in view of her expensive post-war reconstruction; but against the gloomy background of spiralling costs and mounting deficits her running expenses were unacceptable, and it was decided to withdraw her at the end of the season. The author recalls his last sail in her – an unexpected but pleasant evening run to Dunoon and Hunter's Quay – in September when, by strange chance, her call at the latter pier was the last to be made by a Clyde steamer, as it was closed at short notice that very night. A last trip on a favourite paddle steamer, the end of an old pier, the close of a connection between Craigendoran and the Holy Loch dating back a century – they are all symbolic of the end of a way of life familiar to many generations of west of Scotland people, but part of inevitable change in the face of altered transport patterns.

The *Jeanie Deans* lay in harbour for some months before being purchased for service on the Thames; but a brave venture begun there in optimism ended in failure and the final withdrawal of the ship, under the unfamiliar name *Queen of the South*, in 1967. She was towed to Belgian shipbreakers and there, in 1968, ended her eventful career. One does not dwell on the last unfortunate months in alien waters, but we remember instead her last voyage on her native Clyde, sailing down the firth in the red, white and black colours again, in the winter of 1965.

13

MACHINERY AND BOILERS

Just as the twelve vessels described in this book represent the gradual improvement of paddle-steamer design over a period of seventy years, so also did the machinery which drove them exemplify corresponding mechanical development during that time. From the simple oscillating engines of the *Iona* to the modern triple expansion machinery in the *Jeanie Deans*, most of these installations were typical of contemporary practice not only in Scottish waters but also further afield. The principal exception, the tandem arrangement used in the *Duchess of Fife*, was a successful variant characteristic of the Caledonian fleet and deserves attention as an unusual and ingenious attempt to achieve high thermal efficiency with a minimum of capital outlay.

Engineers often developed recognizable styles of their own in the design of paddle engines, and during the 1890s and early 1900s some really beautiful sets were made for Clyde steamers. Not only were the working parts artistically designed, but the painting and decoration of engine rooms was calculated to enhance the overall appearance. The sight of a large, well-designed paddle engine running at full speed was extremely impressive and in this at least enthusiasts of later years had the advantage over their predecessors, for the triple expansion engine of the 1930s and 1940s was considerably more imposing than single and twin crank machinery of earlier days.

Oscillating Engines

J. & G. Thomson, builders of the *Iona* and *Grenadier*, specialised in oscillating engines during the 1850s and 1860s. These were almost invariably of simple expansion type with two cylinders swinging on trunnions through which passed low-pressure steam from the boiler. Several advantages were claimed for this type of machinery. By placing the cylinders immediately below the paddle shaft, all the unbalanced forces of pistons sliding in the cylinders were vertical, thus avoiding the fore and aft surge so noticeable in steamers driven by single diagonal engines. It was a feature not lightly to be discarded in ships employed in long-distance cruising service, and may have been responsible for the anachronistic application of this kind of engine to the *Grenadier* as late as 1885. In an era of cheap fuel the intrinsic inefficiency of the oscillating engine was a matter of little concern, and for some years it held its place as virtually the standard type of Clyde steamboat machinery. Nevertheless, it began to give place to the diagonal engine in the sixties and appeared thereafter only in new steamers built for the Hutcheson and MacBrayne fleet. The *Grenadier* was the last vessel of her class ever to be built with oscillating engines, but in her case an attempt was made to modernise it by making the machinery uniquely of the compound type.

The principle of compounding involves expansion of steam within a cylinder while driving a piston to and fro in the usual way, the steam being thereafter passed at lower pressure and in greater volume to a larger cylinder to repeat the process before passing to the condenser. The improved range of expansion secured thereby leads to higher thermal efficiency, lower coal consumption and, to some extent, firemen's wages for a given mileage; alternatively, for the same running costs, the ship's radius of sailing is increased. It is at least possible that the *Grenadier*, intended for long-distance routes in the West Highlands, had been built as a compound-engined steamer with the latter advantage in mind.

This type of oscillating machinery was never repeated in a Scottish ship. The problem of maintaining steamtight joints in the moving parts was a fundamental disadvantage, made all the more acute by the higher steam pressures of the compound system.

The Diagonal Type

Perhaps the most widely used type of engine in the Victorian period was the single diagonal, a most elementary form of machinery combining robustness with cheapness and simplicity and thus much favoured by proprietors of single steamers or small fleets to whom capital outlay was always a matter of importance. In this type, a single cylinder drove diagonally upwards on to a solitary crank on the paddle shaft from a position low down within the hull, in contrast to similar machinery in contemporary industrial establishments ashore where it was more usual for the cylinder to be placed so as to drive horizontally on to the crankshaft. Early steamers fitted with single diagonal machinery had the slide valve which admitted steam to the cylinder worked by a slip eccentric on the paddle shaft; and reversing had to be done by means of a large lever, assisted if necessary by pinch bars. An illustration of this was the *Lucy Ashton* in her original state, but when the last example of a single engine was built for the *Eagle III* it incorporated a refinement in the form of an auxiliary steam starting-engine. Basically, however, the type of engine had not changed.

The single diagonal was gradually ousted by other types of machinery during the late eighties and early nineties. As ships became larger, they required more powerful engines. Up to a point the 'singles' could be developed to accommodate this trend, although at an ever increasing cost in fore and aft surging as the wholly unbalanced weight of the piston slid backwards and forwards within the cylinder. Such swaying motion became unpleasant after a time and it is noteworthy that other forms of propulsion were invariably incorporated in the best tourist ships of the period. Nevertheless, the type died hard, and its undoubted advantages caused it to be retained for new construction in the North British Steam Packet Company's fleet right up to 1898. Its final manifestation in the *Eagle III* twelve years later undoubtedly reflected her owners' desire to minimise capital outlay.

The simple diagonal engine with two cylinders and a pair of cranks set at right angles enjoyed a limited popularity in Clyde service, and for many years remained the standard form of machinery for Loch Lomond steamers. It was a more expensive installation than the single diagonal engine, but offered considerably greater power without the disadvantage of surging. The *Meg Merrilies*, designed as a fast, cruising steamer therefore required an engine of this pattern, although her owners eagerly reverted to single diagonal propulsion in their specification for a

172

replacement for that ill-starred vessel. The double diagonal engine appeared in only one more Clyde steamer thereafter and it is difficult to understand the initial reluctance of owners to take the logical step forward to a compound version of the same type. Presumably the daunting cost of novel forms of high-pressure boilers and increased maintenance costs deterred them from going over to compounding, for it was generally held that the widely used and inexpensive 'haystack' boiler could not be adapted for high pressures. This proved in time to be an ill-founded supposition.

In the twin crank, compound diagonal engine, Clyde paddle machinery reached its classic form. This most popular and useful arrangement was first employed in the Caledonian steamer *Galatea* in 1889, and in the ensuing two decades became all but standard on the firth. It combined power and thermal efficiency with a minimum of complexity and was incorporated in the largest cruising ships and small general purpose vessels with equal success. Some of the earlier versions, of which the *Neptune* was a notable example, were built with four entablatures (the main engine frames); but the best known arrangement involved a large middle entablature with two lighter ones outside. The designs of the numerous Clydeside engine shops were refined into forms instantly recognizable by the cognoscenti, who could identify at a glance the work of John Brown & Co, Rankin & Blackmore, Hutson & Corbett and other firms in such esoteric details as the outlines of crank webs and entablatures.

The compound engine of the *Duchess of Hamilton* was unique amongst Clyde steamers. She was equipped with a standard set of Denny machinery having Brock valve gear instead of the otherwise universal Stephenson link motion, and in this she resembled several vessels built by the Dumbarton firm for service on the Thames. Brock gear was a marine variant of the Walschaerts valve gear fitted to most modern railway steam locomotives. The valves were operated by a combination of motions derived from the crosshead and a single eccentric, and this pattern of gear required entablatures of a very distinctive appearance, not perhaps visually as attractive as those of more conventional marine engines. Nevertheless, the machinery of the Caledonian flagship was of great technical interest and unusually fascinating to watch in action.

173

Triple Expansion

In the twenty-five years before World War I the Caledonian Steam Packet Company, under the aegis of Captain James Williamson, was foremost in the application of modern forms of machinery to its steamers and it was not surprising that the triple expansion engine made its Clyde début in this fleet. In the triple system, which is a logical extension of compounding, expansion of steam is carried a stage further in a third cylinder and, in its straightforward form, a triple engine has three cylinders of progressively larger diameter driving on to three cranks – an arrangement which became familiar in Clyde steamers of the 1930s. Caledonian paddle steamers, however, were given an ingeniously designed four-cylinder tandem arrangement driving on twin cranks, the patent of the Greenock marine engineers, Rankin & Blackmore. Basically this was an ordinary compound diagonal engine with an extra high-pressure cylinder added behind each of its cylinders, and so arranged that the high-pressure pistons drove on extensions of the piston rods from the larger cylinders. The tandem arrangement on a single crank engine had been much used in earlier Caledonian steamers to give the thermal efficiency of a compound without incurring the capital cost of an ordinary twin crank engine. In the triple expansion version it offered like economies in cost and space, and to all intents and purposes it could not be distinguished from an ordinary compound as the high-pressure cylinders were out of sight.

The first application of this principle had been in the reconstruction of a small twin-screw coasting steamer called the *Arabian*, built by Murray Bros of Dumbarton for Morton & Williamson in the early eighties; and it had been successfully adapted for paddle steamers by Rankin & Blackmore in the *Hygeia* of 1890. The second of two famous excursion vessels designed for service at Melbourne by Robert Morton – we have already noticed the *Ozone* in connection with the origins of the *Duchess of Hamilton* – she attained a speed of 22.8 statute miles per hour on trials and encouraged James Williamson to specify triple expansion engines for Caledonian service in the following year with, however, indifferent success. No other examples appeared for over a decade, and although the *Duchess of Fife*

174

was a highly successful ship her appearance in 1903 marked the final application of this unusual pattern of machinery to a Clyde steamer.

Not until the arrival of the *Jeanie Deans* in 1931 was the Clyde paddle engine seen in its most majestic form. The author remembers vividly the impression made upon him in 1946 when for the first time he saw her large triple expansion engine in action – three large cranks revolving at full speed, long connecting rods flashing up and down, and three sets of valve-gear working steadily alongside the main engines. Gone was the superfine finish of the reciprocating parts of older steamers, and the lining on the entablatures was of the plainest; but the sight of that machinery was awe-inspiring to one whose experience until then had been limited to the pretty little Inglis compound engine of the *Lucy Ashton*. This three-cylinder installation of the *Jeanie Deans* became standard for Clyde steamers of the final generation.

A very similar set of engines was built by Rankin & Blackmore for the last paddle steamer ever built for Clyde service, the *Waverley* of 1947. The same company also supplied an almost identical engine for the *Bristol Queen*, built by Charles Hill & Son Ltd for P. & A. Campbell's Bristol Channel service in the previous year.

Paddle Wheels

By the time of the building of the *Iona* in 1864 the old-fashioned form of paddle wheel with fixed floats had given way to an improved type with feathering floats in all new construction, and such steamers as still retained the obsolete style were being rapidly converted. Feathering paddle wheels had the floats pivoted in bearings in the radial arms and each was actuated by a rod fixed to a bearing in the outside wall of the paddle box, placed eccentrically to the paddle shaft. This simple and effective device allowed each float to enter the water at an acute angle to reduce splashing, turn to a 'full face' position when completely immersed, and leave the water again at an angle so as to minimise the volume of spray lifted by the wheel. It was an incomparably more efficient arrangement than the old wheel, bringing with it the attendant advantages of increased speed for

175

a given power as well as reduced paddle wash, the latter being an important factor in the confined waters of the upper reaches of the river Clyde.

Paddle floats were of wood in the early years but in due course they were largely superseded by steel, said to give increased speed. The *Iona* was one of several ships refitted in this way in the latter part of their careers. The North British company and its successor, the London & North Eastern Railway, clung to elm floats to the end, however, as these were cheaper to replace in the case of damage. Further, in the event of their being smashed by a floating object, they were more likely to break up without causing damage to the structure of the wheel itself. Paddle steamers were always vulnerable to mishaps of this nature and the Craigendoran owners may well have preferred to sacrifice a marginal improvement in efficiency for the more certain benefits of lower cost and repair bills, operating as they did in a great commercial waterway in which floating debris was more commonly encountered than in remoter shipping lanes.

Most paddle steamers had eight floats on each wheel but the two *Duchesses* described in this book typified Caledonian practice in having only seven. Preference varied between one and two strengthening rings, and neither arrangement could be shown to have a decided advantage over the other. Wrought iron gradually gave way to steel as a material during the last years of the nineteenth century; but the use of the latter, although a stronger metal, brought with it increased risk of failure through crystallisation and consequent fatigue.

Boilers

By the 1850s, the typical Clyde steamer boiler was of 'haystack' type. A variety of earlier designs had gradually evolved into this popular form, which enjoyed a wide vogue until the introduction of more modern boilers eventually drove it into decline during the nineties. The adoption of compounding and triple expansion, involving higher steam pressures, was chiefly responsible for the abandonment of the 'haystack' by many owners, for it was essentially a low-pressure steam generator and, in its primitive form, working in conditions of natural draught, thermally inefficient. Nevertheless, its compensating advantages of reliability, lightness, cheapness, and the rapidity with which steam could be raised, commended it in certain fleets for years after competitors had changed over to newer types of boiler. Robert Darling, secretary and manager of the North British Steam Packet Company, was one of the staunchest advocates of its use and argued persuasively against the Caledonian policy of spending large sums of money on what he regarded as unnecessarily expensive machinery and boiler installations.

During the nineties Hutson & Son of Kelvinhaugh Engine Works, Glasgow, developed an improved form of haystack boiler suitable for higher pressures, as did A. & J. Inglis of Pointhouse; and these firms were responsible for the revival in its use about that time. Its construction became a specialised job, the *Marine Engineer* noting that 'the arrangement and preparation of parts are such as to preclude the ordinary run of boiler makers from undertaking work of the kind. The amount of flanging, curvature, and smithing of parts is very great, and is of such a character as to necessitate hand work entirely'. In later years, however, the old skills were largely lost, and when the *Eagle III* came in for possible renovation in 1945 after war service the impossibility of providing a new haystack boiler at an economical price doomed the ship to premature withdrawal.

The brothers Campbell, themselves Clyde men, specified improved haystack boilers for their famous Bristol Channel fleet until the turn of the century. The *Westward Ho*, built in 1894 and engined by Hutson & Son, was the first paddle steamer to combine a haystack boiler with compound machinery, and she and her newer sisters *Cambria* and *Britannia* were acknowledged to be amongst the finest examples of the excursion class in British coastal waters. On the south coast, the magnificent *Balmoral*, built for the Southampton, Isle of Wight & South of England Royal Mail Steam Packet Company as late as 1900, was of similar type; while her rival in the fleet of Cosens & Co, the Inglis-built *Majestic* of 1903, provided a unique combination of a haystack boiler with a triple expansion engine.

In the west of Scotland, and after a long adherence to navy boilers, David MacBrayne's conversion to the haystack type in the reconstruction of the *Iona* in 1891 appeared as something of a *volte face*, but it was well justified by results. When the *Columba* was rebuilt with two massive Hutson haystacks in

1900 instead of the four horizontal boilers originally installed, the ship gained immensely in speed and efficiency, while the saving in fuel amounted to approximately seven tons of coal per day during July 1900 as compared with the corresponding month in 1899. Such practical economies amply supported the similar conversion of the *Grenadier* three years later.

The navy, or horizontal, boiler was of the fire-tube type as used in railway engines – cylindrical in shape, and with cylindrical furnaces. It thus differed radically from the haystack type which, in essentials, was a primitive form of water-tube boiler, with a much larger grate area in proportion to its volume than the navy boiler. The latter was superior at high pressures and was favoured on that account by the Caledonian and Glasgow & South Western companies, being used invariably in closed stokeholds under forced draught to ensure constant steaming conditions. Most vessels had two navy boilers, but the extra size and power of a ship such as the *Duchess of Hamilton* called for three while, conversely, only one was required in the last reconstruction of the *Meg Merrilies*.

The large paddle steamers of the twentieth century usually incorporated double-ended boilers with twin uptakes and funnels, both placed forward of the paddle boxes. The balanced effect of a 'fore and aft' position, exemplified in earlier vessels such as the *Iona* and the *Grenadier*, was lost; but the exceptionally beautiful outlines of the well known Bristol Channel steamers *Gwalia* and *Devonia*, of 1905, showed that the later style need not be aesthetically detrimental. The *Jeanie Deans* was never such a beauty as these ships, but her two funnels in LNER colours made for a most impressive appearance. Her double-ended boiler was essentially a navy boiler doubled, with return flues so designed as to carry the hot gases and other products of combustion back to the uptakes above the furnace doors.

Reference to forced draught calls for a word of explanation. The earliest steamboats depended upon tall funnels to assist in creating strong draughts through their boilers, thus aiding combustion and maintaining steam pressure. A later refinement, during the period when boilers and machinery were boxed in under hurricane decks and saloons, was the provision of large ventilators. These could be rotated to face into a breeze, thus increasing the flow of air into the boiler room and through the fire. In conjunction with the low-pressure haystack boilers of earlier times, such ventilators amply sufficed, and the North British company relied on them for many years as did the Loch Lomond owners and David MacBrayne. The classic arrangement of four large galvanised-steel ventilators clustered round the base of the funnel could be seen on the *Lucy Ashton* until her withdrawal, and the last example finally disappeared only when the *Prince Edward* was broken up after the 1954 season.

Despite the simplicity and cheapness of this system, it was too dependent upon the vagaries of the weather to permit consistent steaming with the high-pressure boilers of the nineties. Even some of the older ships suffered in this respect, perhaps the most notable example being the *Meg Merrilies,* a notoriously capricious 'steamer' in the early part of her eventful Clyde career. In an effort to remedy matters she was converted to the forced-draught system in 1887. This involved sealing off the boiler room to ensure airtightness, and providing double doors to prevent any escape of air and consequent risk of the fire blowing back. A fan was provided to force air into the sealed compartment, raising the atmospheric pressure and ensuring a constant draught through the boiler at all times. While being costlier than the natural-draught system, the combination of closed stokehold and forced draught not only guaranteed steady steaming but also minimised wear and tear of the boiler itself due to fluctuations in draught and temperature. It became universal for modern boilers, during the present century, and gradually ousted the older system.

Condensers

Paddle engines, unlike railway locomotives, did not pass exhaust steam from the cylinders to the atmosphere, save in the very early years. It was invariably condensed and returned to feed water with the object of reducing fuel consumption, for maintenance of a vacuum within the condenser – steam turning to water is much reduced in volume – tended to improve the range of expansion of steam through the engine and so improve thermal efficiency.

First to evolve was the jet condenser, the principle of which was that a jet, or spray, of sea water was passed into the exhaust steam in the condensing chamber, lowering its temperature and converting it to warm water which was in due course returned to the boiler to recommence the cycle. The main disadvantage of this form of condenser was corrosion, or 'pitting', of the boiler plates and tubes due to the presence of salt water, and during the eighties and nineties there was a general trend towards replacement of jet condensers. A more elaborate type was adopted, known as the surface condenser, in which cold sea water was pumped round a nest of tubes through which passed exhaust steam. This prevented contamination of the condensate and prevented damage to the boiler.

In fresh-water conditions, of course, the jet condenser was under no disadvantage and it held its own on Loch Lomond where it worked well with the pure, soft water. Condenser pumps were normally worked by arms and bell cranks from one of the crossheads but later practice, exemplified in the case of the *Jeanie Deans*, was to provide an independent steam pump which secured maximum vacuum in the condenser immediately on starting the main engine.

Colours

Paddle engines were painted in a variety of colour schemes, particularly in the high noon of the Scottish railway fleets in the quarter of a century before World War I. Moving parts – such as cranks, connecting and eccentric rods, expansion links, crossheads and condenser pump arms – were of polished steel, kept bright by constant use of emery; but the cast-iron or steel entablatures (the main frames supporting the crankshaft bearings) had a coarser finish and were painted. Many colours were used, but green or black were most commonly favoured in latter years, with or without plain lining. In earlier days, however, it was common to paint the upper section of the entablature in a darker colour, the lower part being white or cream. Another variation was to paint the inside surfaces in relieving colours.

Lining and elaborate decoration was widely employed in the older ships, and the *art nouveau* designs of the Glasgow & South

Western steamers were unusually striking. The *Duchess of Fife*, last survivor of the Caledonian fleet of pre-1914 years, carried a lion rampant on the middle entablature until her withdrawal from service, but she was the last in a long line. The final examples of elaborate decoration, like many other older practices, were to be found aboard Loch Lomond steamers; the splash plates – placed forward of the cranks to prevent oil from being thrown onto the engine-room walls and deck – being distinguished by intricate designs in red, cream, green and black. The *Prince Edward* was the last ship to carry them in service.

When that pretty and well-loved little vessel passed from the scene, so too did the classic Scottish paddle steamer of the pre-1914 period with her beautiful lines, bright livery and a host of features which had characterised the type for over a lifetime. Not least important of these were the mechanical perfection of her machinery and the interest attaching to her obsolete haystack boiler, once a commonplace in Scottish waters. It could not be said of ships of her class that they exemplified the most advanced marine-engineering practice, save perhaps in their own special field; but to generations of passengers on pleasure bent, the sight of a paddle engine, resplendent with bright paintwork, brass, copper and polished steel, was the image which instantly came to mind and was identified with the proud slogan, 'Clyde built'.

APPENDIX I

Extracts from Specification of the Paddle Steamer *Jeanie Deans*

General   The vessel is to be built and equipped in all respects in conformity with the . . . Specification . . . and also in conformity with the Merchant Shipping Acts and Board of Trade Regulations necessary for the obtaining of Certificates Nos. 3, 4 and 5 for as many passengers as the vessel can be measured for. The scantlings of the vessel to be sufficient for the Board of Trade requirements for Limited Steam 2 Certificate for a 10 hours daylight service between Glasgow and the Isle of Man, 1st June to 31st August inclusive.

Scantlings
All scantlings throughout the vessel to be to Board of Trade requirements. No shell plating below main deck to be less than $\frac{5}{20}$ inch thick.

Bulwarks
The bulwarks to be of steel sheets or plates all round. The frames of the vessel to be carried up to support promenade deck.

Web Frames
Strong web frames are to be fitted under paddle shaft in continuation of outer bearing brackets and main engine bearing beams, also in way of engine and boiler spaces to approved plan. Number and positions of these to be arranged to form continuation for sponson brackets.

Sponsons and Sponson Stays
Paddle beams to be of extra strong build. Bracket plates top and bottom to be carried fore and aft one frame space, carrying plate underneath to be of corresponding type. First stay forward and aft of paddle brackets to be of girder type and carried out to face plate. Remainder of sponsons to be supported by strong iron stays riveted to ship's sides and sponsons through flat palms on ends. Carlings to be of extra heavy type and to be well bracketed on outer and inner sides with gusset plates full depth of face plate; outer gusset should extend

inboard well below line of winghouses. The whole to be tied with heavy stringers and angles fore and aft. Spring beam of American elm. Sponsons of Scotch or English elm; wingwales of English elm. The belting in front of wingwales and ogees to be of elm and to project at least 9 inches from face of paddle boxes. This belting to be kept square. Broad covering steel plates $\frac{1}{2}$ inch thick for top and bottom of fore and aft sponsons of port and starboard sides to be bolted through sponson beams and ogees. The belting to be approved and faced with steel bar 6 inches by $1\frac{1}{4}$ inches tapered at fore and aft sponsons to depth of belting. Suitable accommodation ladders for small boats to be fixed on aft sponsons, and a gangway to be made on each sponson.

Sponson Decks
To be laid on steel angles and beams projecting from ship's side. Planks to be bolted down through angles and paddle beams. Knees of angles at ship's side to be deep enough to take at least three rivets under main deck.

Paddle Boxes
The framing and covering of paddle boxes to be of steel angles and steel plating not less than $\frac{1}{4}$ inch thick. Outer rim angles to be 3 inches by 3 inches and to have plate 9 inches deep riveted thereto; paddle-box facings to be attached to this.

Carving
Paddle-box carving to be in keeping with the name of the vessel, and highly artistic in character.

Engine Framing
Scantlings to be made of extra strength. All rivet holes in connection with these to be absolutely fair, and the greatest care to be taken in the riveting of same, to prevent the slightest working from the motion of the engine. The frames under engines and boiler to be spaced 24 inches centre to centre; first three frames fore and aft engine and boiler compartments to be also 24 inches from centre to centre. Bulb angle frames to be fitted throughout. Intercostals to be carried fore and aft under engines and boiler on each side of and including keelson and to be continued for four frame spaces forward and aft of engine and boiler compartments.

Captain's House
A handsome house of teak panelling and framing with approved obscured glass windows to approved pattern to be placed on

promenade deck immediately forward of stair leading to fore saloon. This house to be sufficiently large to form both sleeping room and office for master. To be fitted with bed, sofa, drawers, writing desk, wash cabinet, and all fittings necessary including window curtains and to be well ventilated.

Boats and Davits

Wood boats, built of yellow pine, with teak top strakes are to be fitted to suit the requirements of the Board of Trade. Davits are to be fitted with cast steel sockets and fixed in such a manner that the boats may be readily swung out, sizes to meet the Board of Trade latest rules. The davits are to be of such a length that when the boat's keel is in position on the ship there shall be at least 2 feet between the blocks. The blocks for the boats to be treble above and below, fitted with gun-metal sheaves.

Decks

Promenade deck The promenade deck to overlap aft end of saloon two feet to shelter end windows of saloon, and to extend the full breadth of the vessel to the stem. Deck to be of 4 inches by $1\frac{3}{4}$ inches teak.

Quarter deck The main deck aft of after saloon to be raised to level of bulwarks and to be enclosed all round with galvanized iron stanchions and rods, and on top a neat teakwood rail. This deck to carry a steam capstan for which provision must be made. Deck to be of 4 inches by $1\frac{3}{4}$ inches teak.

Main deck To be of 4 inches by 2 inches best Oregon pine, except in way of boiler and engine room, which is to be of 4 inches by 2 inches teak. The planks to be free of knots, shakes, sap or any blemish whatever; to be fastened with galvanized bolts; afterwards thoroughly caulked with three threads of best oakum and payed with "Kauxeme" marine glue (R. Bowran & Co. Ltd., manufacturers), and when vessel is finished to be well cleaned, planed smooth and the Oregon pine deck to be served with two coats best copal varnish.

Lower deck Cabin floors to be laid in white pine 1 inch thick, tongued and grooved. All bearers and supports to be of angle iron.

Telegraphs

Three Chadburn's or other approved make telegraphs from captain's bridge to engine room, also docking telegraph from captain's bridge to fore and aft and amidships.

Mast

A pine mast having all necessary fittings, the ironwork and stays, shrouds, etc, all to be galvanized.

Coal Bunkers

Coal bunkers having total capacity of 35 tons to be arranged as shewn on plan. Coal scuttles to be fitted in promenade deck at suitable positions.

Cementing and Painting

During construction, the hull, inside and outside, to be thoroughly coated with two coats genuine red lead. The bottom of engine and boiler spaces to turn of bilge to be covered with best Portland cement or bituminous or other approved composition. The bunkers and sides of hull in stokehold to be coated with hot bitumen. After completion, the outside bottom of hull to get one coat preparatory and two coats approved anti-fouling composition, carried fully 12 inches higher than load waterline, and above the compositions a white line, 2 inches deep running fore and aft parallel with draft line. Above white line, the hull to receive one coat best black paint, and one coat best enamel black, and paddle boxes picked out with gold leaf, and two lines of gold to be run all round the bulwarks. Inside of bulwarks at waist and forward, also alleyways to half their height, to be painted brown, and get two coats varnish. Winghouses and outsides of saloons to be panelled with two coats colour similar to winghouses of steamer 'Waverley'. Inside of winghouses two coats of white paint. Ceilings of aft dining cabin, aft sitting saloon, ladies' tea room, ladies' cabin, all to be polished plywood. Outside of engine house to be painted brown and get two coats varnish, and inside painted two coats white. Other parts of hull, cabins, etc., to be painted and finished to approval. The boats to get two coats of best oil paint, both inside and outside, and to be finished to approval. All painting work to be done on one priming coat.

Machinery Specification

General Description The vessel is to be propelled by a three crank triple expansion surface condensing diagonal steam engine with all pumps independently driven. The engines are to be of the most modern type, well fitted and with all the principal bearings adjustable. Steam is to be supplied by a double-ended boiler of the cylindrical return tube type arranged to burn coal with the closed stokehold system of forced draught and of ample capacity.

The installation is to be designed for a working pressure of 180 lbs.

per square inch and the quality of the various materials is to be in accordance with first class practice for vessels of the type and is to comply with the requirements of the Board of Trade.

Cylinders

The cylinders are to be separate castings of hard close grained cast iron free from defects and finished to the following dimensions:

H.P. cylinder	26 inches diameter
M.P. cylinder	$41\frac{1}{2}$ inches diameter
L.P. cylinder	66 inches diameter
Stroke	60 inches diameter

The H.P. and M.P. cylinders are to be fitted with piston valves and a separate liner is to be inserted in each valve casing. The L.P. cylinder is to have a valve of the Andrews & Cameron type fitted with a cast iron saddle.

Each end of each cylinder is to be fitted with an escape valve of ample size complete with guard and spring and a drain cock at the cover and operated by suitable gear from the starting platform. Receiver pipes which form a pocket are to be fitted with a drain having an automatic steam trap. Indicator cocks are also to be fitted to each cylinder and starting valves to the M.P. and L.P. receivers. The glands for the piston rods and valve spindles are to be fitted with United States metallic packing, those for the H.P. and M.P. being of the high pressure duplex type and for the L.P. of the atmospheric duplex type. The cylinders and casings are to be lagged with non-conducting composition and neatly covered with sheet iron screwed with snap-headed brass screws.

Piston Rods and Crossheads

The piston rods are to be forged steel fitted into the pistons and crossheads on cones and secured by nuts. The crossheads are also to be of forged steel fitted with bronze shoes faced with white metal.

Connecting Rods

The connecting rods are to be of forged steel having double bushes of bronze fitted to a forked end next the cylinders and with a single bearing of brass lined with white metal at the crank pin end.

The bearings are to be secured by steel bolts and nuts and forged steel caps.

Shafting

The shafting is to be hydraulic forged of mild steel manufactured by the Siemens' process and the dimensions are to conform with the requirements of the Board of Trade for Certificate No. 3. The shafts are to be hollow and the crankshaft of the built type. The paddle shafts are to be connected to the crank shaft by solid forged couplings fitted with bolts which are to be secured in one coupling flange by taper and nut and the holes in the other flange are to be lined with hard bronze, and arrangements made for lubricating them.

The paddle shafts are to be fitted into the paddle centres on a cone with feather and nut.

Paddle Wheels

The paddle wheels are to be on the feathering principle each having eight floats of elm.

The paddle centre, eccentric bracket and strap are to be of cast steel, the arms and radius rods of wrought iron and the rim, stays and float bracket levers of mild steel 28–32 tons tensile secured with fitted bolts and double nuts.

The bearings are to be lined with bronze and arranged to facilitate repair and renewal.

The working drawings of the paddle wheels are to be submitted for approval.

Boiler

The boiler is to be of the cylindrical return tube type, double ended, having three furnaces in each end united in three combustion chambers common to the respective pairs of fore and aft furnaces.

Mean diameter	14 feet 0 inches
Mean length	18 feet 6 inches
Internal diameter of furnaces	3 feet 5 inches
Length of bars	6 feet 6 inches
Type of furnaces	Deighton Gourlay
Total heating surface	about 4,000 square feet
Total grate area	136 square feet

The boiler is to be designed, constructed and tested in accordance with the Classification requirements for a working pressure of 180 lbs. per square inch.

The pressure parts are to be constructed of steel manufactured by the Siemens-Martin process, except the tubes, which are to be of wrought iron, $2\frac{1}{2}$ inches external diameter, the plain tubes being swelled $\frac{1}{16}$ th at the front end, and the stay tubes are to be screwed into both back and front tube plates. The tubes are to be fitted with spiral retarders.

The circumferential shell plating is to be in three strakes

longitudinally, and arranged so as to remove all longitudinal seams from the bottom of the boiler.

Funnels

The funnels are to be of suitable diameter and height, made of iron plates $\frac{1}{8}$ inch thick and having an outside casing $\frac{1}{8}$ inch thick. The outside casing is to be butt jointed and flush riveted, the rivets being arranged in vertical rows from top to bottom. Wire rope stays, with stretching screws, to be fixed to eyebolts on the funnels and on deck.

A damper is to be fitted in each funnel with gear controlled from the stokehold floor.

The waste steam pipe is to be carried to the top of one funnel and fitted with a drain led to the feed tank.

Condenser

A surface condenser of Uniflux type having a cooling surface of about 1,600 square feet is to be fitted below the guides to receive the main and auxiliary exhaust steam. The tubes are to be of aluminium bronze manufactured by the Yorkshire Copper Co. Ltd. or other approved maker.

The body of the condenser is to be made of steel plates and angles and the doors and waterway of cast iron.

Doors for inspection and cleaning are to be fitted in the steam and water spaces.

Water Service

Water service pipes with brass cocks and nozzles are to be fitted close to the main framing for the supply of cooling water to crank pins and main bearings.

Main Bearings, Standards and Guides

The main bearings are to be of brass lined with white metal carried in cast steel standards and secured by steel covers and steel bolts and nuts. The standards are to be supported by the engine seating and firmly attached to the structure of the main deck. They are also to be attached to each other by steel stays with nuts.

A forged steel column is to be fitted between each bearing standard and the cylinders, the columns being formed to provide a guide surface for the crosshead shoes.

The column between the H.P. and M.P. cylinders and also between the H.P. and L.P. cylinders are each to form double guides and those on the outside of the M.P. and L.P. cylinders single guides.

Valve Gear

The eccentric sheaves are to be of steel or cast iron and the straps of forged steel lined with white metal. The eccentric rods, quadrants, quadrant block, drag links and way [sic] shaft are to be of forged steel fitted with brass bushes secured with steel covers, bolts and nuts.

The reversing engine is to be of the steam hydraulic type manufactured by Brown Bros. and controlled from the starting platform.

Whistle

One 4 inch organ whistle is to be fitted to the forward side of the forward funnel controlled by a lanyard from the bridge, and fitted with a suitable drain.

Painting

The engines after being cleaned down are to get three coats of the best oil paint and two coats of best copal varnish. The finishing to be stripped as and if required. The boiler when tested and before leaving the works is to be thoroughly dried, cleaned out and to receive two coats outside of the best pure and unmixed red lead oil paint.

APPENDIX 2

Costs of Building the Paddle Steamer *Duchess of Fife* (exclusive of boilers and machinery)

Iron and steel	£1,009	1	8	Boat outfit	£130	0	10
Smiths and mechanics	152	10	7	Spars and rigging	89	7	11
Shipwrights	974	15	5	Deck machinery	731	4	0
Joiners	991	9	9	Anchors and chains	52	0	0
Cabinet makers	43	3	6	Cooking apparatus	81	10	0
Special cabin fittings	41	5	8	Lighting outfit	128	16	3
Patternmakers	43	0	2	Upholstery outfit	365	13	6
Brasswork	220	15	2	Nautical instruments	43	11	6
Tinsmiths	44	1	2	Signals	23	0	6
Coppersmiths	60	12	2	Chandlery stores	20	10	6
Sheet-iron workers	30	8	8	Launch	5	0	0
Ventilation	24	19	2	Trials	26	3	11
Pumping and draining	204	17	10	Fees	52	10	5
Painting	242	16	2	Sundries	69	13	7
Cementing	82	14	6	Expenses at end of season	47	15	0

Total cost of building the ship amounted to £6,038 9s 6d, boilers and machinery being additional to the above.

APPENDIX 3

Financial Costs of Running Caledonian Steam Packet Company Paddle Steamers

	Duchess of Hamilton		Meg Merrilies	
Year ended on 31 December	*1892*	*1893*	*1892*	*1893*
Receipts	£	£	£	£
Cash collected on board	756	711	859	862
Steamer proportion of through bookings	2,032	2,425	1,826	2,475
Goods freights	61	57	236	150
Mails	—	—	62	38
Charters	135	418	20	46
Steward's department (profit)	—	158	—	—
Other collections	185	229	8	3
	£3,169	£3,998	£3,011	£3,574
Expenditure				
Salaries and wages	1,612	1,482	1,197	1,102
Agents	68	57	146	167
Repairs, maintenance and renewals	1,084	993	1,107	1,151
Coals (including porterage)	1,503	1,212	1,569	1,358
Oil, waste and general stores	235	169	203	163
Advertising, printing and stationery	468	265	120	97
Harbour and light dues	359	345	298	284
General expenses	135	255	114	150
Claims and damages	109	3	3	3
Charters and boat hire	61	165	—	20
Steward's department (loss)	168	—	90	61
	£5,802	£4,946	£4,847	£4,556
Balance Working Loss	2,633	948	1,836	982
Add Overheads				
Insurance	411	416	214	184
Depreciation	2,843	2,843	1,178	1,178
Interest	1,097	894	361	344
Loss for the year	£6,984	£5,101	£3,589	£2,688

COMPARATIVE STATISTICS

Year ended on 31 December	Duchess of Hamilton			Meg Merrilies		
	1891	*1892*	*1893*	*1891*	*1892*	*1893*
Number of days in service	118	139	134	253	259	246
Number of miles run	13,583	17,009	16,550	26,067	25,968	23,681
Number of passengers carried	88,731	67,295	68,308	92,621	95,863	115,728
Earnings for the year	£4,405	£3,169	£3,998	£3,801	£3,011	£3,574
Working expenses	£5,617	£5,802	£4,946	£5,349	£4,847	£4,556
Operating cost per mile, including repairs	s d 8 3¼	s d 6 9¾	s d 5 11¾	s d 4 1¼	s d 3 8¾	s d 3 9½
Earnings per mile	6 5¾	3 8¾	4 10	2 11	2 4	2 11½
Cost per day, including repairs, insurance and interest, but exclusive of charge for depreciation	£61 5 5½		£46 13 8½		£20 18 8¾	
		£52 10 10		£23 9 2		£20 8 5¼

Note: Readers are reminded that 240 old pence (20 shillings of 12 pence) are the equivalent of 100 pence under the modern decimal system, but that no valid comparison can be made with present day costs. The above statistics are of interest principally as an illustration of the respective costs to the Caledonian Steam Packet Company of operating two quite different paddle steamers during the early 1890s.

SUMMARY

The statistics illustrate clearly the unremunerative nature of the Caledonian service on the Ardrossan–Arran station, and the impact made upon the company's traffic by the Glasgow & South Western Railway's new steamers in 1892. That a ship of the capacity of the *Duchess of Hamilton* should have carried, during the summer of 1891, an average of only 750 passengers per day suggests under-employment by any standards. When the figure fell to 480 in the following year and it is recalled that the South Western steamer *Glen Sannox*, a larger and more expensive ship, probably attracted a similar traffic, the lavishness of the combined service is seen to be quite unjustifiable, even allowing for the profitable holiday peak traffic.

The figures for the *Meg Merrilies*, referring to the ship in her original form with simple expansion engine and haystack boiler, indicate that she too was uneconomical to operate. Nevertheless similar steamers fitted with navy boilers and compound machinery were then being run profitably, and this suggests that the Caledonian Company's repeated attempts to improve the otherwise modern *Meg*

Merrilies were fully justified. She was employed largely on the Loch Long and Holy Loch routes from Gourock, involving frequent calls at piers situated close to each other and, as a useful maid of all work, was in service about twice as long in each year as the *Duchess of Hamilton*.

APPENDIX 4

Summary of Paddle Steamer Information

Type	Name	Built/Broken up	Builders/Engineers	Home-trade Owners	Dimensions	Boilers	Machinery	Remarks
Iron	Iona	1864 1936	J. & G. Thomson, Govan	David Hutcheson & Co 1864–79 David MacBrayne 1879–1905 David MacBrayne Ltd 1905–28 David MacBrayne (1928) Ltd 1928–34 David MacBrayne Ltd 1934–6	255.5ft × 25.6ft × 9.0ft	Reboilered 1875 2 haystacks, 1891	Horizontal type 50½in × 51in	2-cylinder oscillating
Steel	Chancellor	1880 ?	R. Chambers & Co Dumbarton (1) M. Paul & Co, Dumbarton (2) Blackwood & Gordon, Port Glasgow	Lochlong & Lochlomond Steamboat Co 1880–5 Lochgoil & Lochlong Steamboat Co 1885–91 Glasgow & South Western Railway 1891–1901	199.7ft × 21.1ft × 8.2ft	Haystack, 50psi Navy, 1892, 125psi	(1) Double diagonal, 36in × 60in (2) Compound diagonal, 26in and 48in × 60in	Compounded in 1892 Sold off Clyde in 1901
Iron	Meg Merrilies	1883 1921	Barclay, Curle & Co, Whiteinch (1) Builders (2) A. & J. Inglis, Pointhouse	North British Steam Packet Co 1883 Builders 1884 Captain Robert Campbell 1885–8 Caledonian Steam Packet Co Ltd 1889–1902	210.3ft × 21.4ft × 7.2ft	2 haystacks, 50psi 1 haystack, 1888, 50psi 2 navy, 1897 (second-hand) 2 Haythorn water-tube in 1898, 200psi 2 navy, 1900	(1) Double diagonal, 43in × 60in (2) Compound diagonal, 24in and 43in × 60in	Compounded in 1898 Sold off Clyde in 1902

	Name	Years	Builder	Owner	Dimensions	Boiler	Engine	Notes
Steel	*Grenadier*	1885 1928	J. & G. Thomson, Clydebank	David MacBrayne 1885–1905 David MacBrayne Ltd 1905–28	222.9ft×23.1ft ×9.3ft	2 navy, 95psi 2 haystacks, 1902, 95psi	2-cylinder compound oscillating, 30in and 58in ×51in	Burned out at Oban in September 1927
Steel	*Lucy Ashton*	1888 1949	T. B. Seath & Co, Rutherglen (1) Hutson & Corbett, Kelvinhaugh (2) A. & J. Inglis, Pointhouse	North British Steam Packet Co 1888–1902 North British Railway 1902–22 London & North Eastern Railway 1923–47 British Transport Commission 1948–9	190.0ft×21.1ft ×7.2ft	Haystack, 50psi Reboilered in 1901 Haystack, 1902, 110psi Reboilered in 1923	(1) Single diagonal, 52in×60in	Compounded in 1902
Steel	*Duchess of Hamilton*	1890 1915	Wm Denny & Bros, Dumbarton Denny & Co, Dumbarton	Caledonian Steam Packet Co Ltd	250.0ft×30.1ft ×10.1ft	3 navy, 120psi Reboilered in 1906	Compound diagonal, 34½in and 60in ×60in	Sunk on war service
Steel	*Neptune*	1892 1917	Napier, Shanks & Bell, Yoker D. Rowan & Son, Glasgow	Glasgow & South Western Railway	220.5ft×26.0ft ×9.2ft	2 navy, 115psi Reboilered in 1912	Compound diagonal, 33in and 62in ×60in	Sunk on war service
Steel	*Waverley*	1899 1940	A. & J. Inglis, Pointhouse	North British Steam Packet Co 1899–1902 North British Railway 1902–22 London & North Eastern Railway 1923–40	235.0ft×26.1ft ×8.4ft	Haystack, 110psi Reboilered in 1920	Compound diagonal, 37in and 67in ×66in	Sunk on war service

Type	Name	Built/Broken up	Builders/Engineers	Home-trade Owners	Dimensions	Boilers	Machinery	Remarks
Steel	Duchess of Fife	1903 1953	The Fairfield Shipbuilding & Engineering Co Ltd, Govan	Caledonian Steam Packet Co Ltd	210.3ft × 25.0ft × 8.5ft	2 navy	Triple expansion tandem (4 cylinders) (2) 16½in, 35in and 52in × 54in	
Steel	Eagle III	1910 1946	Napier & Miller Ltd, Old Kilpatrick A. & J. Inglis Ltd, Pointhouse	Buchanan Steamers Ltd 1910–19 Williamson-Buchanan Steamers Ltd 1919–35 Caledonian Steam Packet Co Ltd 1935–6 Williamson-Buchanan Steamers (1936) Ltd 1936–43 Caledonian Steam Packet Co Ltd 1943–6	215.0ft × 25.1ft × 8.1ft	Haystack	Single diagonal, 52in × 72in	
Steel	Prince Edward	1910 1955	A. & J. Inglis Ltd, Pointhouse	Dumbarton & Balloch Joint Line Committee 1910–33 Group Committee No 4 of London, Midland & Scottish Rly and London & North Eastern Rly 1933–47 British Transport Commission 1947–55	175.0ft × 22.1ft × 6.0ft	Haystack	Compound diagonal, 26in and 48in × 48in	

Steel	*Jeanie Deans*	1931	The Fairfield Shipbuilding & Engineering Co Ltd, Govan	London & North Eastern Railway 1931–47	250.5ft × 30.1ft × 8.7ft	Double ended, 180psi	Triple expansion, 3 cylinders, 26in, 41½in and 66in × 60in
				British Transport Commission 1948–51			
		1968		Caledonian Steam Packet Co Ltd 1951–65			
				Coastal Steam Packet Co Ltd 1965–8			

ACKNOWLEDGMENTS

In preparing this book I have drawn on various sources of information which I now acknowledge with pleasure. Mr George Barbour and his colleagues of the Scottish Record Office, Edinburgh, have given me much assistance over a period of several years and have granted permission to quote from the minute books of the Scottish railways and steam packet companies, which form an invaluable source for researchers into transport history.

Another major source, which continues to throw fresh light on the story of steam navigation in the west of Scotland, is that of contemporary newspapers. The importance of these records can hardly be over-emphasised, and I have been most fortunate in enjoying the assistance of Mr J. A. Fisher and his colleagues in charge of the Glasgow collection in the Mitchell Library in my native city. It is with much appreciation that I record their help during the writing of this book. I have also enjoyed similar facilities in the Dumbarton Public Library and at the offices of the *Oban Times* on various occasions.

One of the pleasures of researching a book of this kind is the chance encounter which yields unexpected information. In the course of a delightful holiday in Iona many years ago I had the privilege of meeting the late Rev Ralph Morton, of the Iona Community. The arrival of the excursion steamer from Oban one afternoon caused the conversation to turn to coastal shipping and, to our surprise, we discovered a mutual interest in the subject. Thus, by chance, I met the son of Robert Morton whose contribution to Clyde paddle steamer development was so important. By Dr Morton's kindness I am able to include a photograph of his father amongst the illustrations, and I am also obliged to him for information which I have embodied in the text.

My friend Graham Langmuir provided several illustrations from his magnificent collection, as well as checking many points of information from time to time, and I am very much indebted to him for his ready assistance. Mr John Crosby not only supplied photographs but also went to much trouble to give me information relating to his father's war service in the *Eagle III*. Dr Anthony Weir, with whom I have shared an enthusiasm for paddle steamers for more years now than either of us cares to remember, also allowed me to choose from his collection the fine view of the *Prince Edward* in 1952, and Mr A.

Acknowledgments

Fraser very kindly made it possible for me to include the deck view on board the *Duchess of Hamilton* which recalls so vividly the heyday of that fine steamer. My late friend Michael Warren's collection of photographs from the early 1960s was the source of the cover illustration of the *Jeanie Deans*, also included in the text.

As this book was preparing for press, there came the news of the death of John Thomas, whose passing is deplored by his many friends. He it was who first encouraged my ventures in the field of steamboat history, and he had done much to support me during the writing of this volume when at times it seemed to have been overwhelmed by events. That he did not live to see its publication is therefore a matter of the deepest regret to me, and it is hard to believe that no longer will it be possible to rely upon his generous help and advice. May this book in some measure recall the world of the bygone Clyde, in which he took such a lively interest.

A.J.S.P.

BIBLIOGRAPHY

Books and Booklets

Blake, George *John Rutherford Crosby – A Memoir*, privately published by MacLehose, Glasgow, 1946

Brown, Alan *Craigendoran Steamers*, Aggregate Publications, 1979

Duckworth, C. L. D. and Langmuir, G. E. *West Highland Steamers*, Richard Tilling, 1936; revised and enlarged edn, 1950; 3rd edn, further enlarged and revised, T. Stephenson & Sons, Ltd, 1967

Duckworth, C. L. D. and Langmuir, G. E. *Clyde River and Other Steamers*, Brown Son & Ferguson, 1938; revised and enlarged edns, 1946 and 1969

Galbraith, Rev William C. *Sixty Years of the Lucy Ashton*, Clyde River Steamer Club, 1948

Galbraith, Rev William C. *Sixtieth Anniversary of the Caledonian Steam Packet Company*, Clyde River Steamer Club, 1949

Grimshaw, G. *British Pleasure Steamers*, Richard Tilling, 1945

Hope, Iain *The Campbells of Kilmun*, Aggregate Publications, 1981

MacArthur, Iain C. *The Caledonian Steam Packet Co. Ltd*, Clyde River Steamer Club, 1971

McQueen, Andrew *Clyde River Steamers of the Last Fifty Years*, Gowans & Gray, 1923

McQueen, Andrew *Echoes of Old Clyde Paddle Wheels*, Gowans & Gray, 1924

Paterson, Alan J. S. *The Victorian Summer of the Clyde Steamers (1864–1888)*, David & Charles Ltd, 1972

Paterson, Alan J. S. *The Golden Years of the Clyde Steamers (1889–1914)*, David & Charles Ltd, 1969

Somerville, A. Cameron *Colour on the Clyde*, The Buteman, 1958

Stromier, G. M. *Steamers of the Clyde*, Nicholson, 1967

Thornton, E. C. B. *South Coast Pleasure Steamers*, T. Stephenson & Sons Ltd, 1962

Williamson, James *The Clyde Passenger Steamer from 1812 to 1901*, James MacLehose & Sons, 1904

Bibliography

Technical

G. E. Barr 'The History and Development of Machinery for Paddle Steamers', Paper read to the Institution of Engineers and Shipbuilders, Scotland, 1951

Files of *The Engineer, Engineering, The Marine Engineer, Marine Engineering*, and *The Shipbuilder*

Source Material

Scottish Record Office, Edinburgh
    Minutes of the Caledonian Steam Packet Co Ltd
    Minutes of the North British Steam Packet Company
    Minutes of the North British Railway
    Minutes of the London & North Eastern Railway
    Minutes of the Glasgow & South Western Railway
    Minutes of the Dumbarton & Balloch Joint Line Committee
National Maritime Museum, Greenwich
    Denny Collection – engineering records
University of Glasgow, Department of Economic History
    Denny Collection – business records

Newspapers and periodicals
The Ardrossan & Saltcoats Herald
The Bailie
The Buteman
The Dumbarton Herald and Lennox Herald
The Glasgow Herald
The Greenock Telegraph
The North British Daily Mail
The Oban Telegraph
The Oban Times
and several other Clyde coast newspapers of the period

Miscellaneous
The Wotherspoon Collection, The Mitchell Library, Glasgow
Records of the Clyde River Steamer Club, Glasgow

GENERAL INDEX

203

INDEX OF STEAMERS
AND OTHER VESSELS